Creating a Customer-Centered Culture

Also available from Quality Press

At the Service Quality Frontier
Mary M. LoSardo and Norma M. Rossi

Quality Service Pays
Henry L. Lefevre

Deming's 14 Points Applied to Services
A. C. Rosander

Implementing Quality with a Customer Focus
David N. Griffiths

Quality Dynamics for the Service Industry
W. F. Drewes

Quality Service—Pure and Simple
Ronald W. Butterfield

The Customer Is King!
R. Lee Harris

The Quality Revolution and Health Care
M. Daniel Sloan and Michael Chmel, M.D.

Quality Assurance in the Hospitality Industry
Stephen S. J. Hall

Quality Management in Financial Services
Charles A. Aubrey II

To request a complimentary catalog of publications, call 800-248-1946.

Creating a Customer-Centered Culture

Leadership in Quality, Innovation, and Speed

Robin L. Lawton

ASQC Quality Press
Milwaukee, Wisconsin

Creating a Customer-Centered Culture:
Leadership in Quality, Innovation, and Speed
Robin L. Lawton

Library of Congress Cataloging-in-Publication Data

Lawton, Robin L.
    Creating a customer-centered culture: leadership in quality,
innovation, and speed / Robin L. Lawton.
        p.   cm.
    Includes bibliographical references (pp. 165–68) and index.
    ISBN 0-87389-151-1 (acid-free paper)
    1. Customer service—Quality control.   2. Total quality
management.   I. Title.
    HF5415.5.L39   1993
    658.8'12—dc20   93-15572
                                                      CIP

Creating a Customer-Centered Culture™ and The Customer-Centered Culture Model™ are trademarks of International Management Technologies, Inc. Time: Systems™ is a trademark of Time Systems, Inc.

10 9 8 7 6 5

ISBN 0-87389-151-1

Acquisitions Editor: Susan Westergard
Production Editor: Annette Wall
Marketing Administrator: Mark Olson
Set in Caslon 540 and Gill Sans by Montgomery Media, Inc.
Cover design by Montgomery Media, Inc.
Printed and bound by BookCrafters, Inc.

ASQC Mission: To facilitate continuous improvement and increase customer satisfaction by identifying, communicating, and promoting the use of quality principles, concepts, and technologies; and thereby be recognized throughout the world as the leading authority on, and champion for, quality.

For a free copy of the ASQC Quality Press Publications Catalog, including ASQC membership information, call 800-248-1946.

Printed in the United States of America

♾ Printed on acid-free paper

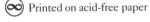

611 East Wisconsin Avenue
P.O. Box 3005
Milwaukee, WI 53201-3005

To my parents, David and Jean,
who taught me to appreciate both the
power and the subtleties of language.

Contents

Acknowledgments

Many people have helped to make this book possible. Most important among them are my customers. All of them have been leaders who were intrigued by my ideas and believed that radical change in their organizations was not only possible but necessary for survival. In many cases, their support for my concepts, methods, and proposals entailed substantial personal risk for them. We often joked that their efforts had "career-limiting potential" because they were bucking the trend of conventional thinking within their organizations. In spite of whatever initial obstacles they encountered, they achieved success and sometimes hero status.

These people are not shy, retiring wallflower types, which meant that just as they challenged their own organizations, they continually raised their expectations of me. Their relentless striving for perfection has helped me develop my message and its deployment process so that it works under every condition where we've applied it.

Special thanks are due to Carlton Braun, a corporate vice president at Motorola. Carlton is the creator of the Motorola Management Institute, a vehicle for educating executives, managers, and professionals in the new competencies required to advance Motorola's worldwide leadership. Carlton first met with me in 1986 to invite my participation in his efforts. His suggestions, criticisms, and encouragement since then have given me a personal appreciation for Six Sigma Quality (99.99966 percent perfection).

Bruce Rismiller is also especially appreciated. Bruce had been an executive at Xerox and Carson Pirie Scott before he joined Northwest Airlines in 1990 as a senior vice president. Bruce challenged me to demonstrate at Northwest that knowledge workers could apply my approach with the level of result I said was possible. Our many after-hours discussions helped me to appreciate the magnitude of the transformation he was trying to achieve and the many things he was doing to model the new behaviors he expected of others. He greatly contributed to my ability to articulate the new paradigm described in this book.

Larry Whobrey is a example of what a midlevel person can do to create a successful transformation process, in spite of significant obstacles. Larry is responsible for the quality initiatives in a large service division of Caterpillar. His contribution was to let me help him set up a transformation process with very little personal on-site involvement on my part. Larry's demand for just-in-time training left him alone to devise a new training delivery system. The traditional training folks couldn't (or wouldn't) accommodate him. His creativity has prompted people in other divisions to ask for his help in their own initiatives.

Other customers I have especially appreciated include Jim Krattenmaker at Honeywell, MaryAnn Stump at Blue Cross/Blue Shield, George Wollner at the U.S. Department of Labor Statistics, and Phil Lundblad at the University of Minnesota.

In addition to customers, my colleagues at International Management Technologies, Inc. have been invaluable in preparing this book. I would first like to thank Linda Logan, my business partner since 1985, for her creative contributions to this work. Special thanks go to Carol Goehner for her desktop publishing talents and to the rest of the team for keeping the ship afloat while I siphoned off time to write. Last, but not least, my wife Melinda has my appreciation for her support and advice during this project.

If this book helps you in pursuing your leadership initiatives, all the folks above must share the credit. If it does less than you want, I own responsibility.

Introduction

There is no longer any debate about the importance of quality in determining economic success and organizational longevity. The 1980s taught us this on several levels: nationally, organizationally, and personally. A quality renaissance is now underway among manufacturing organizations. The challenge facing most managers in the 1990s is how to apply formal quality management methods appropriately to those of us who do not make widgets. According to the U.S. census, over 70 percent of us are in service work both within and outside of manufacturing organizations. We could argue that all of us have a knowledge or service component to our work.

During the 1980s, many publications shared the successes of selected companies in addressing quality and customer satisfaction. Books like *In Search of Excellence* by Tom Peters and Bob Waterman, *Service America* by Ron Zemke and Karl Albrecht, and *Total Quality Control: The Japanese Way* by Kaoru Ishikawa described what others had done and tried to distill the principles that led to success. They created excitement and enthusiasm. They shared a vision of what was possible. Unfortunately, understanding the principles is much easier than actually implementing them.

Others offered their own specific Holy Grail as *the* solution for achieving total quality. Many of these solutions have attempted to transfer manufacturing-based quality methods to knowledge and service work. For example, the conventional thinking by many within the quality movement is to become "best in class" by focusing on continuous improvement, zero defects, statistical process control, and massive training. The organizations using these approaches as their total quality management (TQM) strategy can expect both bad news and good news.

The bad news:

- None of these management methods helped slide rule makers produce calculators; or the typewriter makers achieve leadership in word processing software, or camera producers develop VCRs.
- Improvement does not guarantee survival.
- Problem solving is not the same as leadership.
- Only a tiny percentage of the people who are trained in quality methods actually use them.
- Current TQM approaches are based on ideas which were new in the industrial age of the 1950s.

That was then.

The good news:

- Your competitors may still be using the conventional wisdom. If so, they may become the defect-free buggy whip makers of the future.
- You don't have to throw out the old to adopt the new.
- Hype, jargon, and mass training are unnecessary to achieve a dramatic, sustainable transformation quickly.
- The new concepts and tools outlined in this book are so compelling and intuitively appealing, you'll wonder why you aren't already using them.
- The new leadership strategy is based on the needs of the information and service age of the twenty-first century.

This is now.

Traditional quality management solutions proven effective by manufacturing organizations have often been applied as stand-alone remedies, with the assumption that they apply equally well to knowledge and service work. If it were that easy, we wouldn't continue to see the two- to three-year death-and-rebirth cycle of quality initiatives. A recent *Wall Street Journal* arti-cle[1] cites a study by McKinsey & Co. which found that two-thirds of quality programs had either stalled or failed to produce real improvements.

Many organizations have encountered difficulty transfering the methods and technologies developed to address manufacturing quality for use in knowledge/service work. This book addresses how to do just that. The primary focus is on creating a new conceptual framework that changes the way we think. This change in thinking places heavy emphasis on the language we use to describe reality and our relationship to it. Our language reveals our values. Those values affect behavior. Our experience has been that examining and changing our language will confront us with our current values, enabling us to assess their impact on creating desirable outcomes. The new thinking provides a context for using both the traditional and emerging quality management tools to address customer satisfaction. Mastery of the new thinking will make subsequent actions possible, at both a personal and a strategic level.

The purpose of this book is to provide a proven, practical approach to achieving and sustaining leadership in quality and customer satisfaction for knowledge and service work. The concepts, strategy, and tools have been used by many organizations, including Motorola (a user since 1987 and a Malcolm Baldrige Quality Award winner), Blue Cross/ Blue Shield, Caterpillar, Northwest Airlines, U.S. West, Target Stores, government agencies, and many others. The emphasis will not be on what these organi-zations have done but on what you can do both personally and within your organization.

You will be disappointed if you are looking for all the answers to be laid out. Many are, but I have found that it is impossible to tell someone how to think differently. The change in thinking occurs most often when personal experience demonstrates a change is necessary; then the change occurs naturally. This book has been designed to lead you through that experiential learning process. Completing the exercises in each chapter will enhance your experience and understanding. However, this book cannot instill the same level of insight or mastery as you would achieve during live interaction in our workshops.

The sequence and design of the chapters and exercises is intended to provide you with what we could call progressive revelation. This may not exactly be a religious experience, but the insights and enlightenment you obtain should have a noticeably positive impact on you, your organiza-tion, and your customers.

Everything in this book is aimed at helping you achieve specific outcomes, reflected in understanding the answers to these five key questions for yourself and your organization.

- *What* do we do?
- *Who* do we do it for?
- What do they *want* and why?
- How can we better *improve* their satisfaction and our performance?
- What is the *strategy* and *process* for creating a customer-centered culture?

For any book to have practical relevance and cause change, it must first connect with our personal experience. It may be helpful to share with you my own first experience with initiating quality and productivity changes in a service environment. I do this to introduce certain concepts we'll expand on later and to show that radically improved organizational performance can occur in spite of daunting obstacles to change.

It all began for me in 1972 when I started work at the Jackson State Prison in southern Michigan. I had graduated the year before with my B.A. in sociology and was eager for a chance to "make a difference." The position offered to me had just been created by a federal grant. I was to be responsible for supervising the academic, vocational, and psychological intake testing program for all convicted male felons in the state of Michigan. Based on the results of these tests, medical evaluations, the nature of the crimes, and other factors, these men received a "classification recommendation" and were sent to receiving facilities across the state to begin serving their sentences.

This maximum security correctional facility was euphemistically called the Reception and Guidance Center (RGC). It was an appendage to the largest walled prison in the country (at that time). The RGC consisted of two 500-man cell blocks. One was for inmates under 23 years old, the other for those older.

The working environment was not great. Aside from the cockroaches and mice which would dart across my desk, there were periodic inmate fights to contend with.

Like many new employees in organizations everywhere, I had been given the briefest of orientations to my new work. And since the position itself was new, I was pretty much left to myself to figure out what needed to be done. After I had been on the job a few weeks, several things became clear:

- The inmates were spending 60 to 90 days at the RGC even though much less time was required to complete the assessment activities.
- The assessment and testing processes managed by the different organizational functions were poorly coordinated with each other.
- The RGC was intended as a temporary housing facility, and little recreational activity was available. Since there was so much time spent waiting for the next scheduled event, the enterprising inmates were creative in finding things to do—such as victimizing each other.

My experiences during my first six weeks on the job, along with a strong belief in the power of logic and reason, prompted me to offer a proposal to the facility's top manager on how to streamline the intake process. The manager's response went something like this: " I've been here for seven years, and things were fine until you arrived." This began my introduction to the political realities of change and how logic and reason alone are no match for the entrenched status quo.

Fortunately, I was able to find a champion for my proposal who had connections with others in power. To make a long story short, about a year later we had achieved or were well on our way to the following successes.

- The intake process was cut from more than 60 days to 15 days, a reduction of 75 percent of the total cycle time.
- All operations were moved into one cell block, cutting facility and related capital and staffing requirements almost in half.
- Most of the internal documents were consolidated, redesigned, or eliminated to improve simplicity, quality, and productivity.
- Victimization occuring during waiting time had been greatly reduced.
- Major changes in job duties, staffing, and structure had begun.

What I did not know at the time was that many of the improvement methods I used are similar in concept to manufacturing-based quality methods such as quality loss function, statistical process control, just-in-time, quality function deployment, value analysis, poka-yoke, and time-based management. Neither my colleagues nor I had ever been exposed to these technical disciplines. Our ability to achieve significant change in this tough-to-change environment shows that these gains are possible for anyone.

My mission is to demystify these issues and reframe how you think about and manage knowledge/service quality. This reframing may differ from conventional thinking in several ways.

- Service quality is *not* customer service (although customer service and customer relations are a part of service quality).
- Although manufacturing-based models and techniques for managing quality can produce some improvement, they may be more hindrance than help in applying quality management strategies to knowledge and service work. Jargon must be removed and an appropriate sequence of methods be applied to achieve rapid customer-centered transformation. Appropriate language usage can speed the introduction of change. Even when technical jargon (that is, SPC, QFD, JIT, CQI, QWL, and so on) is avoided, words like *service* and *customer* require explicit definition.
- Even the most advanced TQM methods and techniques will have limited impact until the values, producer-centered measurements, and incentives that promote our organizational culture are transformed into customer-centered ones.
- Significant change in customer satisfaction and cultural orientation can occur without initial massive training efforts.

The material covered in this book is appropriate for the uninitiated and the experienced quality management practitioner alike, regardless of organizational position. My emphasis will be on applying this quality leadership system to your own specific situation. To do this, I'll provide brief exercises after each major concept is introduced. These will not only reinforce the concepts but also will provide examples that you can use immediately in your own work. My objective is to provide you with the concepts, methods, and processes for building a quality-conscious culture that focuses on outcomes desired by customers.

The Customer-Centered Culture Model™ is the conceptual framework for all the ideas addressed in this book. The model (see Figure I-1) shows the relationships among seven major topics (outcomes, mission, source products, process, product, attributes/expectations, and customer).

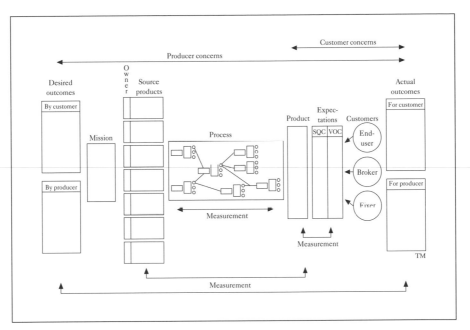

Figure I-1: The Customer-Centered Culture Model™.

The customer-centered culture *strategy*, distinct from the model, is described in Chapter 7.

The model is not a flowchart reading from left to right. It can be used that way, but it is primarily intended to show relationships, not sequence. We could begin with almost any of the seven topics and show its relationship to the other items. For example, most of the current TQM initiatives in the United States focus primarily on process. Although this book will address process, we have very strong evidence that process is not the most effective place to begin the quality journey. The reasons should be clear by the time you have completed Chapter 2.

The actual sequence we'll use to address the five key questions mentioned earlier is shown in Figure I-2. These concepts are easy for most people to understand. Their simplicity initially can mask their depth of meaning and their power to enable radical change. Completing the exercises in each chapter is the only way you can truly uncover this depth and power.

Based on the experiences of thousands of others who have used or been exposed to the model, you can reasonably expect to pass through the

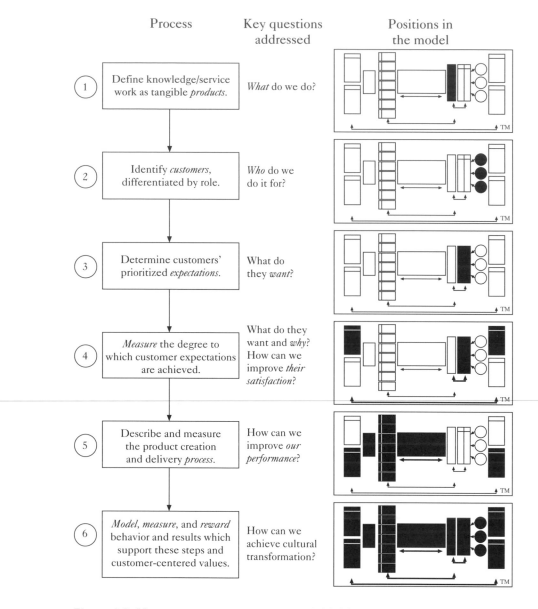

Process	Key questions addressed	Positions in the model
① Define knowledge/service work as tangible *products*.	*What* do we do?	
② Identify *customers*, differentiated by role.	*Who* do we do it for?	
③ Determine customers' prioritized *expectations*.	What do they *want*?	
④ *Measure* the degree to which customer expectations are achieved.	What do they want and *why*? How can we improve *their satisfaction*?	
⑤ Describe and measure the product creation and delivery *process*.	How can we improve *our performance*?	
⑥ *Model, measure*, and *reward* behavior and results which support these steps and customer-centered values.	How can we achieve cultural transformation?	

Figure I-2: How to create customer-centered thinking.

upper right pane of the Johari window in Figure I-3. The four panes describe the stages of learning or development we all experience.

If you and I were to meet, initially I would not know anything about you. I wouldn't know how to best communicate with you. I would be in the lower right box: unconscious incompetence. Sometimes this stage in our

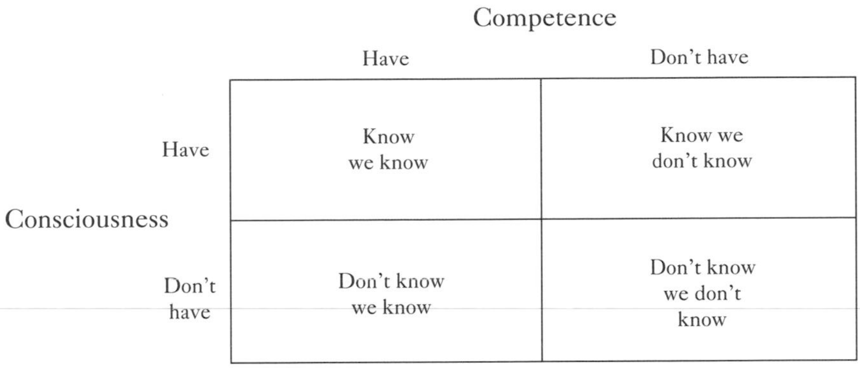

Competence

	Have	Don't have
Have	Know we know	Know we don't know
Don't have	Don't know we know	Don't know we don't know

Consciousness

Figure I-3: Stages of development: the Johari window.

development can be akin to "ignorance is bliss." Since I won't know about your likes and dislikes, I may feel confident that my general ability to get along with others will be sufficient to establish a relationship with you.

As we get to know each other, we will find out things about each other that we didn't know. I may be surprised to find that assumptions I had about some of your likes are not correct. This new awareness puts me into the upper right box: conscious incompetence. The bad part about being in this box or position is that I may inadvertently do something that displeases you and find out after the fact. The good thing is that the discomfort I feel as a result of your displeasure can motivate me to change. A satisfying relationship can develop as we become increasingly conscious of our mutual interests, needs, and challenges. We work to arrive in the upper left box: conscious competence.

People who have known each other for a long time sometimes drift into the bottom left box: unconscious competence. You and I could do the right things by each other out of habit. This can work out fine until I need to explain to someone else how to develop a good relationship with you.

The first three stages will be particularly relevant to your experience with the topics covered in each chapter. Expect to feel some discomfort as you pass through the upper right box on your way to an increased sense of conscious competence.

I wish you a satisfying journey.

Notes

1. "Quality Programs Show Shoddy Results," *Wall Street Journal*, 14 May 1992.

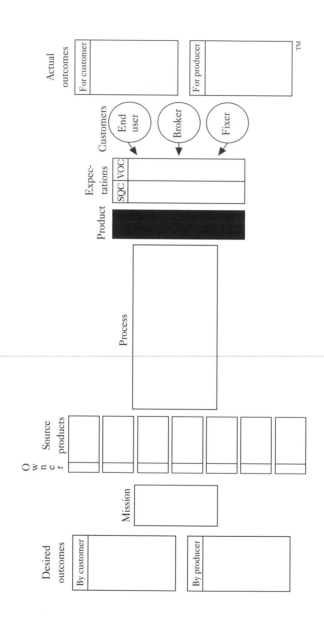

The Customer-Centered Culture Model™

1

The Service Product

I've always been fascinated by how revealing our social rituals are. They can illustrate our values, the way we define ourselves, and the world view we share with others.

One simple ritual we've all experienced occurs at large social gatherings: company picnics, professional conferences, large family reunions, or even dinner parties. Consider the most recent such event that you attended. If there were people there you didn't know, how did they introduce themselves to you?

One of the ways we break the ice in these situations is to ask others about themselves. A common question is, "What do you do?" If you are like most people, you probably gave a response similar to one of these: "I'm the vice president of sales at Hi-Tech, Inc. I help our regional offices with their sales strategies and large client relationships," or "I'm the personnel manager at Global Media. I do all the recruiting for new technical and management positions," or "I'm a nurse at Town Center Hospital. I work with the oncology and cardiac patients," or "I'm a customer service representative at Financial Services, Inc. I handle customer complaints, get statements corrected, and help our customers get answers." These statements contain three parts: (1) our role or position, (2) our organizational affiliation, and (3) our work activity.

So why is this important? Understanding this common ritual is important in understanding how we define our primary roles, relationships, and priorities. Being conscious of the ways we describe ourselves makes it possible to improve. If we can do this on a personal level, we can transfer the learning and skills to changing our culture. Just as we may define ourselves in terms of our role, affiliation and activity, we will use the same thinking to describe our culture.

In working with thousands of professionals in hundreds of organizations, I have found that over 95 percent tell me they are in knowledge or service work. When I ask them what they mean by "service," they offer a great variety of definitions. These definitions reveal a lack of consensus about what service means.

Our first major challenge in creating a customer-centered culture is to define what we do in a way that lets us manage and measure it. The word service has a fuzzy meaning. Even though most of us would say we perform service work, it can be difficult to define what that means. Think of the various ways we use the word:

- Customer service
- Medical service
- Lip service
- Emergency service
- Repair service
- Financial service
- Consulting service
- Military service
- Creative service
- Social service
- Postal service
- Information service
- Religious service
- Secret service
- Engineering service

What is a one-word definition of service? Most people have a hard time answering that question. Two of the most common definitions of service are "help" and "assist." Do these words reflect proactive or reactive action? If you initiate the assistance, it is proactive. If you provide it in response to a request, it is reactive. Both words imply reactive, not proactive, behavior. Even though service can be either a verb or noun, we are inclined to think of service as a verb—an activity. So service turns out to be something which is hard to define, represents activity, and is reactive.

Unless we do something about the way we think of service, it will be mighty tough to manage it under these conditions, let alone measure how well we're doing it.

The labels we use for organizational functions reinforce our concept of service as activity. Engineering, purchasing, shipping, marketing, accounting, data processing, advertising, and training all refer to activity. When we embark on improvement of an activity, we look at changing how we do what we do (process). While this seems logical and reasonable, it misses the basic fact that customers generally don't care how we do our work. This focus on our own activity encourages producer-centered thinking.

Problems with "Service"

- Lacks shared meaning
- Treated as activity
- Performed reactively
- Misplaces priority on "how"

Customers do care about what we provide to help them achieve some desired outcome. These things are products. Products (expressed as nouns) are deliverables. They are countable, occur in discrete units, have names we can make plural (with an s) and often occur as some form of packaged information. There are two types: manufactured products and knowledge/service products. General types of service products include the following:

- plans
- procedures
- processes
- reports
- repairs
- designs
- answers
- manuals
- invoices
- strategies
- financial statements
- courses
- policies
- presentations
- recipes
- greetings
- deliveries
- contracts
- diagnoses
- orders
- referrals
- specifications
- consultations
- systems
- proposals
- diagrams
- meetings
- schedules
- programs
- transactions
- audits
- connections

Tables 1-1 and 1-2 show examples of service products, organized by function and by industry.

A service product is the tangible deliverable produced by work activity. An individual or work group's principal product is the deliverable that most closely represents its mission (its purpose). The actual mission statement itself (a product) can include a definition of organizational purpose, a

Function	Sample products	
Executive management	Policies Strategies	Plans Mission statements
Marketing	Brochures Ads Campaigns	Surveys Marketing plans
Personnel	Policies Procedures Processes	Programs Placements Performance reviews
Quality	Policies Processes	Audits Specifications
Training	Courses Manuals	Programs Needs assessments
Sales	Orders Presentations	Plans Needs assessments
MIS/data processing	Installations Reports	Applications (software) Systems
Shipping/receiving	Deliveries	Schedules
Accounting	Reports Audits	Balance sheets Entries
Customer service	Answers Solutions	Connections Referrals
Purchasing	Approved purchase orders Procedures	Authorized vendor lists
Engineering	Designs Layouts Procedures	Processes Specifications Instructions
Field service	Repairs Upgrades	Installations Diagnoses

Table 1-1: Sample products organized by function.

Service industry	Sample products	
Health	Diagnoses Tests Therapies	Prescriptions Treatments Injections
Financial services	Statements Accounts Investments Mortgages	Recommendations Loans Policies
Transportation	Deliveries Shipments	Flights Reservations
Restaurants/hospitality	Meals Lodging rooms	Confirmations Reservations
Entertainment	Movies Shows Rides	Plays Performances Exhibits
Education	Courses Tests Catalogs Programs	Assessments Schedules Grades Degrees
Legal	Statutes Rulings	Opinions Regulations
Retail	Stocked items	Displays
Telecommunications	Connections Directories	Installations Repairs

Table 1-2: Sample products organized by industry.

statement of values that governs behavior, general activities that support the purpose, and boundaries of responsibility. For example, a data processing department could state: "Our mission is to develop and apply reliable and consistent information management technologies to assist management in directing the business." One of this department's main class of products would be software applications.

Products are tangible or concrete. Every product has a producer and at least one customer. The service product is the link between us and our customers, both internal and external.

Service regards *how* we deliver.
Product regards *what* we deliver.

DEFINING PRODUCT

Identification of the service product is essential for creating a customer-centered culture. Identifying service products sounds easy, but your first "reality check" is to identify your own (see Exercise 1).

EXERCISE 1: PRODUCT DEFINITION

A. Write at least four specific products *produced by your immediate work group.* (Do *not* state "information," "answers," or the name of a manufactured product.)

1. _____   5. _____

2. _____   6. _____

3. _____   7. _____

4. _____   8. _____

B. Now identify examples of *products you personally create.*

1. _____   3. _____

2. _____   4. _____

C. Select one of the most important products named in either section A or B. Write the specific name of the product on the line below. Do *not* use "answers" or the name of a manufactured product here.

_____

There are several ways to see if what you've written in Exercise 1 is correct. If you can answer "yes" to the following questions about your product names, you've mastered the first step in customer-centered thinking.

- *Is the product something only you or your immediate work group can claim as yours?* For example, a product name of *policy* or *plan* isn't specific enough to claim ownership. Such labels represent whole classes of products. There are probably others who would also claim those products as theirs. A *personnel selection policy* or a *product development plan* are examples of specific product names only you or your immediate work group might claim as yours.

- *Can you make the product plural?* If the label you wrote is followed by "—ing," it is an activity, not a product. The product is the tangible deliverable that is created by activity. Results like *satisfaction, assurance,* and *security* also are not products. They are outcomes (intangible results or conditions) obtained by using the product.

- *Does the product, as named, occur in countable units? Information* can only be considered as a product by the various forms it takes. Reports, graphs, answers, proposals, plans, and manuals are examples of information products. Information is raw material, delivered to others in some organized or packaged form.

- *Is the product intended to create a desired outcome or result for a customer?* Satisfaction, security, fun, profit, productivity, and knowledge are outcomes your product might create. Some people confuse outcomes with the product itself. A number of executives have told me that their products are *direction* and *leadership*. Their true products include policies, plans, and strategies which, when used by others, propel the organization in a desired direction. These types of products are also called source products. All of an organization's major processes are directed by source products (to be discussed later). The inadequacies or absence of such products can lead to organizational failure. Leadership is a skill or outcome, not a product.

Many people who try to define their products make a number of discoveries. Here are some of the most common, as stated by participants in our workshops.

- It is hard to change our thinking of what we do from activity to deliverables.
- Identifying products focuses us on results.
- Now I know why others have a hard time understanding what I do.
- Most of what I do is intangible.

- Defining my products has made what I do concrete.
- It can be difficult to identify the products we create.
- Products focus on customers.
- We don't usually measure the volume, cost, or quality of our service products.
- We actually produce very few products compared to the amount of time worked.
- The concept of "product" enables me, for the first time, to consider how meaningful measurement can be applied to what I do.
- Once we've identified our products, it is easier to determine correctly who our customers are.
- We have a lot of activity, "product" focuses on results.
- Product focuses on value perceived by customers.
- Product reminds me of my customers.
- A lot of my activities can be organized by product.
- A product must be very specific to identify customer roles.

The understanding of this concept of the service product is absolutely critical to everything else we will address in this book. The real beauty of identifying service products as tangible entities is that everyone has them. Their concreteness also makes them measurable. If you have any doubt about the products you identified in Exercise 1, please stop here. Make sure your products meet all the criteria. Be sure the one you selected in section C is important and will be appropriate to focus on for the rest of the book. Although I'll be using a variety of examples from here on, use your own product to get the most benefit from the application exercises.

I suggest we remove the word *service* from our vocabulary and replace it with *product*. Or use *service product*, if that will help.

We all create dozens of products, either personally or through our immediate work groups. Some are considered stand-alone or finished products, while others are really pieces of a larger product. For example, the main or core product of Northern States Power (NSP), a Minnesota utility, is packaged in the form of kilowatts or kilowatt hours. NSP also has a customer service group that provides answers. Answers can be considered part of the core product, part of the "service" expected by purchasers of kilowatts. Answers also are a class of product produced in response to some stated need. NSP has tried to reduce some of the reactive nature of this service product by providing answers proactively. It periodically sends customers a booklet called "Ask NSP" that identifies over 100 commonly asked questions on such topics as insulation, energy consumption of appliances, and energy conservation. The booklet simply lists each topic and provides a specific phone number the customer can call for a prerecorded answer. A person is also available to answer calls, if necessary. Major reasons to design answers (and similar information products) are to satisfy customers and reduce or eliminate "I don't know" responses.

At first glance, considering answers as important products may seem trivial. It's not. Let's take these concepts and make them personal. If answers are products you give to others, they are probably provided in response to questions. Most of us would prefer to have as little of this reactive activity as possible. I'll share with you an approach to doing just that and simultaneously improving customer satisfaction.

First, we need to collect quickly a little data representing the volume, cost, and quality of your answers. How many questions do you need to answer in a week? The nature of your role and responsibilities determines whether these questions come primarily from within the organization or from outside. Let's suppose that most of the questions come from other departments within the organization, primarily by phone. How many do you get in a week? Most of us are able to give an estimate, but we really don't know. We don't usually count them. If this is true for you, make this (volume of questions) your first data collection task. The reasons will become clear shortly.

Suppose you get 50 questions and provide 50 answers per week. How much of your total work time does this represent? I'm frequently told by managers, supervisors, and professionals that 40 to 80 percent of their time is consumed in trying to provide answers. If so, this is clearly a significant issue. Let's assume that you spend only 40 percent of your time providing answers. This is equivalent to 16 hours (2 days) of a 40-hour week. At $25 per hour, your organization is paying you $400 per week or $20,800 per year to provide answers. This provides the first step in estimating the nontrivial cost of your answers to questions and requests for information. In this simple scenario, each answer costs an average of $8. Use Tables 1-3 and 1-4 to estimate the financial investment made in your answers.

What percentage of your answers are some form of "I don't know" to the caller's first request? Consider that the customer's objective is to get a complete, easily understood, accurate answer on the first attempt. This is the customer's definition of answer quality. Anything less than that is considered an "I don't know" (IDK) by the customer. Unless the customer is calling specifically for a referral, any referral to a third party must be considered an IDK. The same is true for a promise to provide the requested answer at a later time.

Hours per week spent answering questions	Hourly compensation rate (in dollars)									
	$10	20	30	40	50	60	70	80	90	100
5	$50	100	150	200	250	300	350	400	450	500
10	100	200	300	400	500	600	700	800	900	1000
15	150	300	450	600	750	900	1050	1200	1350	1500
20	200	400	600	800	1000	1200	1400	1600	1800	2000
25	250	500	750	1000	1250	1500	1750	2000	2250	2500
30	300	600	900	1200	1500	1800	2100	2400	2700	3000
35	350	700	1050	1400	1750	2100	2450	2800	3150	3500
40	400	800	1200	1600	2000	2400	2800	3200	3600	4000

Table 1-3: Cost of answers per week.

If you don't currently count the number of IDKs you or your immediate work group provides, make this your second data collection task. Organize the IDKs into no more than seven topic categories. One of the categories is labeled "other"; the six other topic categories are determined by your experience in trying unsuccessfully to provide answers on the first request. These seven categories will produce a Pareto chart. It prioritizes IDKs so you'll know which one to focus corrective action on first. The objective is to reduce drastically or eliminate IDKs. These are the first steps in measuring answer quality and preventing customer dissatisfaction.

It is the rare organization that counts IDKs. A major insurance company in Hartford, Connecticut, did. One of its discoveries was that 75 percent of internal calls were not getting to the intended party and that 60 percent of them did not require dialogue. We'll discuss how to use this information shortly.

Total cost of answers per week	Number of answers created per week									
	10	20	30	40	50	60	70	80	90	100
$50	5	3	2	1	1	1	1	1	1	1
100	10	5	3	3	2	2	1	1	1	1
150	15	8	5	4	3	3	2	2	2	2
200	20	10	7	5	4	3	3	3	2	2
250	25	13	8	6	5	4	4	3	3	3
300	30	15	10	8	6	5	4	4	3	3
350	35	18	12	9	7	6	5	4	4	4
400	40	20	13	10	8	7	6	5	4	4
450	45	23	15	11	9	8	6	6	5	5
500	50	25	17	13	10	8	7	6	6	5
600	60	30	20	15	12	10	9	8	7	6
700	70	35	23	18	14	12	10	9	8	7
750	75	38	25	19	15	13	11	9	8	8
800	80	40	27	20	16	13	11	10	9	8
900	90	45	30	23	18	15	13	11	10	9
1000	100	50	33	25	20	17	14	13	11	10
1050	105	53	35	26	21	18	15	13	12	11
1200	120	60	40	30	24	20	17	15	13	12
1250	125	63	42	31	25	21	18	16	14	13
1350	135	68	45	34	27	23	19	17	15	14
1400	140	70	47	35	28	23	20	18	16	14
1500	150	75	50	38	30	25	21	19	17	15
1600	160	80	53	40	32	27	23	20	18	16
1750	175	88	58	44	35	29	25	22	19	18
1800	180	90	60	45	36	30	26	23	20	18
2000	200	100	67	50	40	33	29	25	22	20
2100	210	105	70	53	42	35	30	26	23	21
2250	225	113	75	56	45	38	32	28	25	23
2400	240	120	80	60	48	40	34	30	27	24
2450	245	123	82	61	49	41	35	31	27	25
2500	250	125	83	63	50	42	36	31	28	25
2700	270	135	90	68	54	45	39	34	30	27
2800	280	140	93	70	56	47	40	35	31	28
3000	300	150	100	75	60	50	43	38	33	30
3150	315	158	105	79	63	53	45	39	35	32
3200	320	160	107	80	64	53	46	40	36	32
3500	350	175	117	88	70	58	50	44	39	35
3600	360	180	120	90	72	60	51	45	40	36
4000	400	200	133	100	80	67	57	50	44	40

Table 1-4: Cost per answer.

Before going on, let's summarize the points made so far.

- Answers are an important class of products.
- There is a significant cost incurred to produce answers.
- Customers have the same expectations of answers that they have for any other product: They want what they want when they want it.
- Counting and organizing IDK responses to customer inquiries measures quality and identifies opportunities to become proactive.

How to use Tables 1-3 and 1-4:

1. Estimate the number of hours you spend each week answering questions. This includes time spent understanding the requester's needs, researching possible answers, collaborating with others and communicating the answer.
2. Identify the column in Table 1-3 that best represents your total hourly compensation rate.
3. Locate the intersection of the row (hours/week) identified in step 1 and the column (compensation rate) identified in step 2. For example, if 25 hours/week are consumed at $50/hour, the total cost of answers you create per week equals $1250. This does not include the comparable cost consumed by your customers in obtaining answers from you.
4. In Table 1-4, find the row for the number identified in step 3.
5. Estimate the number of answers you create in a week.
6. The intersection of the row identified in step 4 and the column from step 5 tells you the estimated average cost for each answer you create.

Understanding that answers are products helps us realize that saying "I don't know" is equivalent to being out of stock of important products. The typical hardware business measures its stock of products for two primary reasons: (1) to prevent the loss of sales by making sure sufficient stock is available when a customer wants it, and (2) to prevent overstocking costs. Repeatedly being out of stock on items customers expect guarantees that customers will go elsewhere. If these are good reasons for a hardware business to measure its stock of merchandise, they are equally relevant for measuring our on-hand stock of prepared answers.

I have argued for years that a major reason for the growth of the personal computer business is not because of its wonderful technology. It is because most of us who have worked in large organizations have been frustrated with the lack of responsiveness of the data processing organization. Waiting for over a year to get a new application on the mainframe is unacceptable. It represents an IDK to our request for help. The personal computer helps us get the answers right away.

We need to count our stock of answers for the same reasons the hardware business counts its stock of paint. This is not a trivial pursuit. It will lead to remarkable insights. One common revelation is that people who call us for answers may be calling the wrong people. Why? It could be that they already know us and believe we will help them get to the right person, even though we can't immediately answer their need ourselves. This is both good and bad news. The good news is that we've created a relationship of trust or confidence. The bad news is that we may be so tied up with needs coming to us inappropriately that we're distracted from accomplishing our primary mission.

If the customers don't know us, they may be calling us inappropriately because they don't know who else to call. This is extremely common. Why? One primary source of the problem is the directory the caller is using. We've been discussing a scenario where these callers are internal. That means the caller would be using an internal directory. How is your internal directory organized?

The directory is another product. Most organizations arrange the directory alphabetically by employees' last names. Some will also organize information by functional groups. How does this organization scheme match the customer's organization of thoughts for help? There is usually little or no match. Customers of the directory have to somehow find a match between their specific needs and the person or group to contact. Several of our clients have redesigned their directories by including topics organized by customer needs. The results have included the following:

- Customers get fast, accurate answers on the first try.
- The number of people involved in getting an answer is greatly reduced.
- Departmental workload and costs due to inappropriate requests for help are reduced.
- Costs for on-demand answers are reduced by prepackaging answers in easy-to-use formats (brochures, directories, and so on).

All of this becomes possible by thinking of answers as products and applying the same measurement systems to them that we would for a manufactured product.

We've also seen that answers are only one type of product in a chain of products. The fact that we get any calls for help is usually a sign that something further upstream is not done as well as possible.

The scenario we've worked through involved internal customers. The comparable problems associated with providing answers to external customers are often even more challenging. Yet we could do some simple things to help both ourselves and our customers.

A classic example involves the ubiquitous 800 numbers for customer service. One of the products many of us use in summer is charcoal. We use charcoal for barbecues or grilling at predictable times: evenings and weekends. Some of the charcoal makers seem oblivious to this fact: On the bag of charcoal, next to the 800 number we should call if we have problems or complaints with the product, the published office hours typically are 9 A.M.–4 P.M. EST, Monday–Friday. Is it any wonder researchers find that producers only hear from 4 percent of their unhappy customers?

Typically, products occur in chains. It is important to understand the relationship every product has with products that precede it. For example, a medical treatment would be preceded by a scheduled appointment, examination, diagnosis, prescription, and treatment plan. The final product in the chain—the medical treatment—is the one primarily intended to create a desired outcome for the external customer. In this case, the outcome desired by the patient is a cure. The quality of the final outcome depends on the quality of the preceding products.

In manufacturing organizations, service (information) products always precede a manufactured product. Such service products include marketing plans, forecasts, customer orders, product designs, specifications, and schedules.

Understanding the product chain is important in preventing quality problems. This may seem obvious, but it is surprising how often organizations focus quality improvement efforts on the tail end of the product chain rather than on the front end. The organization's management is primarily responsible for these front-end products, including policies, strategies, plans, and designs. How can we expect employees to create quality final products if the front-end ones aren't right (or even there)?

We can draw these conclusions:

- It is advantageous to define products before addressing processes.
- Products occur in chains.
- Knowledge products always precede manufactured products.
- Product definition is the first step in achieving both customer satisfaction and problem prevention.

Beginning the quality management process with product definition is fundamentally distinct from addressing activities and work processes. Although W. Edwards Deming and others have made major contributions to our ability to improve quality through process management, our love affair with statistical process control (SPC) and other process improvement methods has sometimes been misguided. Deming himself pointed this out in his book *Out of the Crisis*. If the products we create are not what customers want, improving the production process can lead to great efficiencies without necessarily achieving great customer satisfaction.

This is not meant as a criticism of systems for process control. Process management methodologies are an essential component of managing quality. It is simply a critique of our tendency in the United States to adopt a methodology blindly as "the answer." We did this with quality circles in the early 1980s. Problem-solving techniques and process control followed later in the decade as solutions to our difficulties with corporate and national competitiveness. Some relatively advanced readers of this book may consider quality function deployment (QFD) as "the answer." Yet it is only a part of the answer. We so often describe the elephant by the piece we happen to be holding at the moment.

Throughout this book, I strive to integrate these various methodologies and techniques into a coherent system for managing change in quality for the customer's benefit. Some of these recommendations will fly in the face of conventional thinking. But they should still make intuitively good sense, and they are eminently practical to apply.

Product design must precede process design and control. Likewise, the sequence in which we use the various quality management technologies is important in achieving the greatest impact from our change efforts.

If you have successfully defined the most important product that you, or your organization creates, *congratulations!* You have answered the first of the five key questions (see the Introduction) necessary to achieve quality leadership: *What* do we do? We create products.

We're now prepared to answer the second question: *Who* do we do it for?

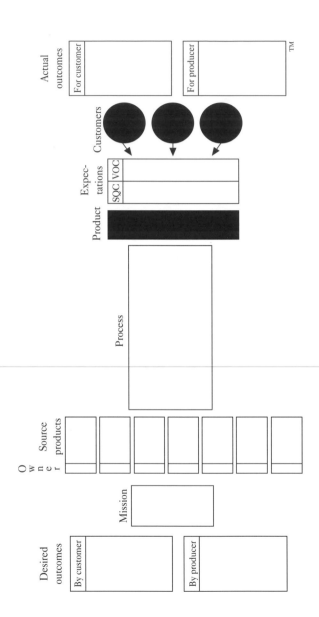

The Customer-Centered Culture Model™

Differentiating
Customers

One of the positive developments in the last several years is the common realization that we all have customers. That's the good news.

The bad news is the conventional wisdom that we have two types of customers: internal and external. At one time, it made sense to introduce the idea of internal customers. This helped those who didn't have relationships with customers to find practical meaning in the customer concept. While it is true that we have internal and external customers, this view dangerously oversimplifies. Essentially it classifies customers by location. There are three problems we must address before going on to a more adequate understanding of customer roles.

The first problem is that a customer relationship is said to exist if there is interaction between two functional groups. Is an internal customer one who is in my department? My division? My discipline? My section? My company? Where are the boundaries between "internal" and "external"? If the purchasing department interacts with the data processing department, who is a customer of whom? How do we know? We can choose to make the easy response that we're customers of each other. What does this accomplish? It might make us feel good about each other, but its fuzziness makes it difficult to take meaningful action. What should data processing do to satisfy its customers in purchasing? The internal/external distinction does little to answer these questions.

The second problem is that an entity might have only internal or external customers, not both. This is usually true of the data processing department if "internal" refers to others within the organization. Whenever this is the case, the internal/external distinction is irrelevant.

The third problem occurs when we have customers with competing needs. This is most of the time. We can easily come to the erroneous conclusion that we know who the most important customers are: those with power which comes from their position, personality, purse strings, or proximity. These four "power p's" can inadvertently lead us to satisfy the wrong customers.

The solution to the first problem is to identify the purchasing department's products. An approved vendor list is one product the data processing department uses. In this case, purchasing is the producer, and data processing is the customer. Purchasing also produces other products (such as purchasing contracts with vendors) for which data processing is not a customer. Conversely, data processing produces a monthly budget statement for the purchasing department. In this case, data processing is the producer, and purchasing is the customer. *The product determines the producer-customer relationship* and is the basis for addressing customer satisfaction.

The only way to solve all these problems and make certain we know who the "right" customers are is to understand their differing roles with specific products. The customer's location or organizational affiliation is of little practical relevance. Customers have three distinct roles that are always determined by the product.

> *Customers' roles are always determined by their relationship with a specific product.*

End-users are individuals or groups who actually use the product to achieve a desired outcome. They are the folks we supposedly had in mind when we designed, created, and delivered the product. For every product, there usually are more end-users than any other kind of customer. This is the most important type of customer.

Brokers transfer the product to someone else who will use it. They may act as an agent of either the end-user or the producer. As an agent of the end-user, the broker makes the product more accessible, easier to use, or more appealing. As an agent of the producer, the broker "encourages" the end-user to accept the product.

Fixers transform, repair, correct, modify, or adjust the product at any point in its life cycle for the benefit of end-users.

The beauty of understanding these roles is that they apply both to internally consumed products (that is, forecasts, budget statements, business plans, technical manuals, procedures, and so on) and to externally consumed products (such as saleable products, contracts, and annual reports).

THE ROLE OF BROKERS

The broker's responsibility is to continuously look for ways to bring the producer and end-user closer together.

The auto industry offers a classic illustration of what can happen when we don't clearly understand customer roles and priorities regarding externally consumed products.

In the mid-1970s, President Jimmy Carter told U.S. automakers that they needed to build fuel-efficient cars. He wasn't saying they had to build him, as an end-user, a fuel-efficient car. He was acting as a broker, an agent of the end-users, in saying that was what consumers needed. American automakers went to the folks who actually buy the cars from them, the car dealers, for their thoughts on the matter. The dealers said, "Send us more of those big babies. We'll sell as many as you make."

Why would they say that? Larger cars generally have bigger profit margins. Whose interests were these car dealers representing? Their own interests and those of the producers, who were not eager to change. The automakers made a common mistake. They were confused about who the most important customers are: the end-users. Since the car dealers are buying the cars from the producers, it is easy to be influenced (sometimes inappropriately) by these broker customers.

Japanese car makers responded differently to President Carter's challenge. They heard him stating a new requirement and worked to address it. They used it as a marketing point. The end-users, brokers, and producers of Japanese cars have benefitted. In fact, Honda's CVCC engine was the first to meet the stringent antipollution standards set by the Clean Air Act of

1970 without requiring a catalytic converter.[1] This helped create Honda's reputation for innovative technology.

These differing responses by the American and Japanese automakers point to the distinguishing features of two types of cultures. A producer-centered culture is characterized by producers and brokers who act in collusion to the disadvantage of end-users. I hasten to add that this is usually not done consciously or with malicious intent. It seems to happen this way naturally when we're not consciously focused on end-users and their needs.

Our objective is to satisfy all the customers of a product, even though their needs are different. If they have competing interests, the producers in a customer-centered culture give preferential attention to end-users over brokers. When producers and their brokers act to the advantage of end-users, everyone wins. If producers and brokers myopically focus on their own concerns, to the disadvantage of end-users, the end-users will still ultimately win; competitors will satisfy their needs. The announcement in late 1991 by General Motors' president that over 70,000 employees were to be laid off illustrates the fate of producer-centered organizations.

Brokers can help reinforce customer-centered thinking or producer-centered thinking. My intent is not to portray brokers as bad people; they aren't. We are all brokers for some product or another. It's just that brokers can have conflicting interests. When brokers express needs for a product to be designed or configured a specific way, these needs must be consistent with what the end-user wants. Those needs are best uncovered by the producer through direct interaction with end-users. Where that is not possible or practical, customer research can help. Producers must understand who their end-user and broker customers are.

End-users always win in the long run.

The auto industry offered an easy example; so do many service industries. The insurance industry presents another classic case of producer confusion about customers. Most insurers openly say their agents are their customers. What are the policyholders, chopped liver? The insurance agents are indeed customers. They are brokers, though, not end-users of the insurance policies. The agents are end-users of the sales compensation plan, sales tools, prospect lists, and other products. But for the insurer's core product, an insurance policy, the policyholder is the end-user.

Why should insurance companies care? To avoid the fate of the U.S. auto industry and to prosper by satisfying policy buyers. Insurance policies are a type of contract. The producers of most contracts are attorneys. The language used in most contracts, insurance policies included, seems best suited for attorneys. The end-users of the policies would be well served by being able to understand them easily.

One service industry that appears to be following in the auto industry's footsteps is network television. TV programs are their core product. A long-standing complaint of the viewers (end-users) is that quality programs don't survive while junk programs take an increasingly large share of network viewing hours. Using our model, we find the explanation for this problem in the role of advertisers. Advertisers act as brokers by funding programs they expect will result in merchandise sales. Who are they representing?

Compare program funding for network TV with that of public TV. In the first instance, advertiser/brokers and producers call the shots. With public TV, the producers receive funding directly from significant end-users. George E. Wollner would call those with the funds "incentive controllers."[2] By confusing the incentive controller (often a broker) with end-users, we get confused about who we really need to satisfy in the long run. One could argue that giving power to end-users has led to the growth of public TV. Conversely, broker-driven network TV continues to suffer from an eroding customer base where no one wins in the long term. My prediction for the past several years has been that cable TV, funded by end-users, ultimately will reduce the networks to minor rivals. The best distribution of power occurs when the end-users are also the incentive controllers.

It is easy for producers to ignore end-user interests inadvertently. Of the three types of customers, brokers generally have the most frequent and intense interaction with producers. This results in brokers having a great deal of influence over the design and distribution of products. This is not necessarily a bad thing, as long as the end-users' interests are faithfully represented by brokers and given priority attention by producers. Unfortunately, it is the rare organization that actively and formally includes users and fixer groups in the design of new products.

Look at the whole enterprise. It may seem obvious that end-users are the final buying customers, brokers include the sales and distribution organizations, and fixers include the field service and customer service people. However, as we discussed at the beginning of this chapter, we must remember that it is actually not organizational membership that determines customer role. Each specific product determines customer roles.

The health care industry offers a good illustration of how complicated customer differentiation can be and why it is essential to consider the specific product in determining roles.

To begin with, some of the players in a medical model of the health care industry include:

- Attending physicians
- Referring physicians
- Accreditation boards
- Patients
- Insurers
- Attorneys
- Nurses
- Government agencies
- Hospitals/clinics
- Patient employers
- Patient advocates

Industry professionals have told me that one of their problems is determining whether the hospital's customers are the doctors or the patients. Those of us who have been hospital patients realize that hospitals carefully cater to the needs of doctors. Traditionally, physicians have been treated with reverence. On the other hand, consider that hospitals call their end-user customers "patients." This disempowering label fosters paternalistic attitudes by providers as well as dependency in patients. There are some who say, "They call us patients because we've got to be." For this industry, the first step in creating a customer-centered culture is to eliminate the term "patients" and begin behavior appropriate to "customers." By the way, another label used by health care is "waiting room." In every other industry, comparable rooms are called lobbies or reception areas. Do you think it is just coincidence that health care uses the terms "waiting room" and "patient"?

The current thinking among some hospital management entities goes like this: The patient goes to a hospital where his/her doctor works; hospitals need patients; therefore, hospitals have to attract and treat doctors well so patients will come to the hospital. Doctors are viewed as key customers.

Another way to determine customer role is to consider their relationship with a specific product. In the sense that the hospital's "product" is a fully equipped operating room, the hospital is the producer and the surgeon is the end-user customer. This is a relatively easy relationship to understand.

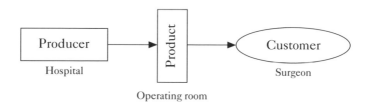

Figure 2-1: Roles when an operating room is the product.

The story is more complicated when the product is an appendectomy. The cast is identified below:

Player	Roles
Patient	End-user (of the appendectomy)
Surgeon	Producer (of the appendectomy)
Referring physician	Broker for the producer and broker for the end-user
Hospital	Broker for the producer and broker for the end-user
Nurse	Broker for the producer and end-user
Patient advocate	Fixer and broker for the end-user
Insurer	Broker for the end-user
Patient's employer	Broker for the end-user
Attorney	Fixer (if malpractice is charged)
Government	Broker for the end-user regarding appendectomy pricing

Figure 2-2: Roles when an appendectomy is the product.

When the appendectomy is the product, the surgeon is the producer. The hospital is the broker for both the producer and the end-user/patient. The insurer (private insurance company or the government's Medicare system) is a broker for the end-user, both in terms of negotiating a pre-approved fee structure for an appendicitis diagnosis and in paying the bill. The employer is a broker for the end-user in terms of insurer selection. The end-user customer is the patient. When the patient is convalescing after the surgery, the nurse may be a broker for both the producer/surgeon and the end-user/patient.

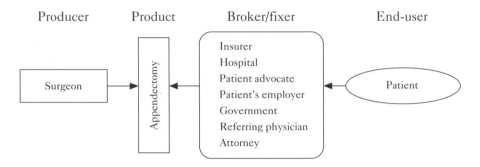

Figure 2-3: Relationships when an appendectomy is the product.

This situation is fertile ground for problems. Let's look at some general problems (and possible corrective actions) that can arise from this situation.

Role Confusion

The broker (hospital) can experience role confusion from trying to serve three competing interests: its own, the producers', and the end-users'. Whenever this situation occurs, there is high potential for end-users' needs to be lost in the shuffle or to receive lower priority (as illustrated by the car story related earlier).

Recommended action: Seriously reconsider Kaoru Ishikawa's assertion that "the next person in the process is your customer." While this is true, the customer could be a broker. To create a customer-centered culture, remember that all other players exist to satisfy the final end-user's interests. The interests of that final end-user must be kept uppermost in mind. It is true that the attending physician is an end-user for the operating room. But that operating room, the physician, and the hospital are irrelevant without the patient. Empower end-users by communicating with them, and by actively identifying and making explicit what their interests are. How to do this will be described in the next chapter.

> *The next person in the process is your customer.*
>
> Kaoru Ishikawa
>
> *The next person in the process is probably a broker.*
>
> Robin Lawton

Too Many Brokers

The sheer number of brokers between the end-user and producer can cause problems. In this brief example, we've got at least five. An extended broker chain can function much like the game of "telephone": A group sits in a line or circle. One person whispers a phrase to the person next to him or her, and it continues around the group. The last person to hear the phrase speaks it aloud. By that time, the phrase usually has been significantly altered from the original statement. Likewise, there is a potential for the end-user's needs to be miscommunicated.

Recommended action: Look for ways to eliminate, consolidate, or automate broker functions. This may involve removing, consolidating, or creating new interim products. The objectives are to reduce time consumption, improve convenience, and maintain clear focus on end-users' interests.

Three strategies for improving the broker function (to be pursued in the order shown) are:

1. Eliminate it.
2. Consolidate it.
3. Automate it.

Mobile surgical facilities and home health care are ways the interim product of the operating room and its producer, the hospital, could bring the final end-user into direct contact with the primary caregiver. A comparable example from the financial services industry is the automated teller machine (ATM). ATMs enable the end-user of a bank account to withdraw cash virtually anywhere, anytime. Tellers only work bankers' hours. ATMs work customers' hours.

An example of a relatively new product that capitalizes on the concepts underlying my recommendations is Prodigy. This is a software-based shopping service offered by IBM and Sears that enables the user to purchase a wide variety of goods and services by computer and phone. For instance, a traveler can quickly find and buy the lowest airfare at the most convenient time, without going through a travel agent; and trading stocks does not require a stock broker.

As we've indicated before, the end-user will win in the long run, no matter what. The broker's responsibility is to look continuously for ways to bring the producer and end-user closer together.

It is the producer's responsibility to give priority to the needs of the end-user. This involves talking with users and those fixers and brokers who represent and work closely with the end-users.

THE ROLE OF FIXERS

The quality director for a tool manufacturer once took me on a tour of his plant. He showed me a felt-lined box of wrenches. The wrenches looked unusual. They had twisted handles. He explained that this box of wrenches was a "new car tool kit." I was surprised to hear this, since the only new car tools I had ever seen before were the jack and lug wrench stored with the spare tire, so I asked him what he meant by "new car tools." He said most new cars manufactured in the United States require these special tools to allow mechanics to fix the engines and other components. Who do you suppose pays for these special tools? We, as end-users, ultimately do. What role do you think the fixers had in the design of the new cars? None.

Fixers interact intensively with end-users. They have a terrific wealth of information about what the end-user experiences using the product. As producers, we can help both ourselves and our end-user customer by capitalizing on what the fixers know. The opportunity is enormous.

A number of years ago, I was working with the field service division of a computer manufacturer. Its 3,500 employees were the corporation's fixers, counterparts to the Maytag repairman. This division's management was one of the first leadership groups in the company to formally address quality management as a strategic issue. The division had been a cash cow for the company. Its profit had grown at about 7 percent per year for the previous two years. Those in management were comfortable with this but also knew they had improvement opportunities.

The first challenge was to identify their core product. Division managers initially told me that I would best understand their work by thinking of the division as firefighters. When a computer went down, their job was to fix it. On the surface, this analogy made good sense. They had defined their core product as a repair. But the more I understood about the division and its priorities, the clearer it became that the thinking represented by the analogy was fundamentally unsound.

Using the analogy, consider yourself the manager of a fire station. What happens to the size of your budget as the number of fires increases? It probably will go up. In most organizations, there is a direct relationship between size of budget and level of the manager of such a budget. This is only one of the many incentives that, in a twisted way, rewards us for more fires.

This was precisely the sort of incentive influencing the division's priorities. Management had also conducted analysis which revealed that the company's major competitor appeared more "productive." It had over 20 percent more repairs per field engineer than my division. Management's response was to require the field engineers to increase the number of calls per day. One could argue that this was like asking the Maytag repairman to make more calls!

The bad news was that management initially refused to redefine the division's core product as "fire-free days" and the desired outcome as 100 percent up-time. The good news was that I was able to assist their enlightenment through the following process.

The first step was to measure the quality of a repair. This is not as easy as it might appear. Imagine taking your car in to the shop because it's hard to start on cold mornings. The mechanic replaces your battery. A month later, the car begins to have the same problem. Was it fixed? Most of us would say it wasn't. The mechanic may swear that that the battery actually needed to be replaced. But on the second trip to the shop, it turns out the battery charging system needed to be fixed, too. Do we count this situation as two repairs or one repair that had to be redone? If the problem didn't reappear for three months, does it change our perception of the quality of the first repair? These are the kinds of issues we had to address with the computer manufacturer. To make a long story short, we were able to define for the first time what a "quality repair" was.

The second step in changing management thinking was to compare the two years of profit growth with repair quality during the same period. The comparison is in Figures 2-4a and 2-4b. These charts immediately make it clear that, even though profit was growing, quality was declining.

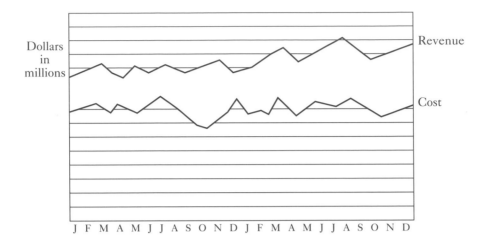

Figure 2-4a: Profit growth.

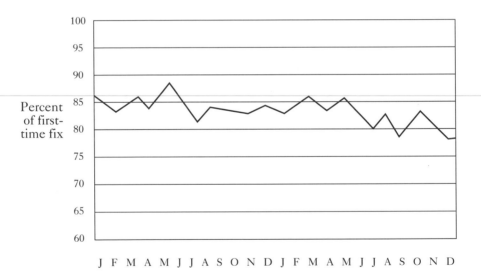

Figure 2-4b: Repair quality.

The trend represented the path to extinction. Management responded to the wake-up call.

The third step was to find out what accounted for the trend. A key source of information was the field engineers. We found that the computers didn't contain effective diagnostic systems to isolate bad components properly, training manuals and tools weren't provided until after machines were shipped to customers, and some parts had high failure rates. The bottom line was that this division, the fixers, had not been formally involved in the product design process. As soon as that change was made, computer quality and end-user satisfaction were on the road to significant improvement.

Including the fixers in product design changes the emphasis from reaction to proaction. The fixers can include functional groups like the field service group or customer service. But the fixer role can also be held simultaneously by those who have end-user, broker, or producer roles. The end-users of a financial report may also have to be fixers if the report has to be modified to be usable. Our challenge as producers is to seek out the fixers and end-users and empower them.

Exercises 2 and 3 will help you identify customer roles for one of the products you identified in Chapter 1.

Conclusion

The following represent the most common discoveries experienced by participants in our workshops.

- The end-users don't have the most power.
- There are many levels of customer.
- Brokers have the most power.
- Communication between producers and end-users is weak and indirect.
- The brokers are the customers we have focused on the most.
- A person or group can have more than one role with a product, even though one is primary.
- Those furthest from end-user customers have the most power.
- It's easy to mistake brokers for end-users.
- Customers can have more than one role.
- Brokers have the *most*, end-users the *least* power.

It is not sufficient to recognize that we all have customers. Understanding the roles customers play with each of our products guides us in prioritizing who we must listen to most closely for success in the long run. Congratulations on answering key question 2: *Who* do we do it for?

We should be creating products for end-users but may actually be focusing on brokers. Chapters 3 through 5 will help you answer the key third question: What do they want and why?

EXERCISE 2: PRODUCT–CUSTOMER RELATIONSHIPS

1. Your target product is _____ .
   Focus on this one product as you answer questions 2 through 6. You may want to
   use the product you identified in section C of Exercise 1.

2. Name the *end-users*
   of this product
   (individuals or groups).

3. Name the *brokers*
   between you and your
   end-user customers,
   if any exist.

   Brokers for end-users {

   Brokers for producer {

4. Who are the *fixers*
   for this product?

5. What is your primary role with this product?

   _____ producer   _____ user
   _____ broker for producer   _____ fixer
   _____ broker for user

6. Now go back and rank the current power of all the customers identified
   in questions 2 through 5 (including yourself).
   Power refers to the ability to direct or change the design of the product
   (1 = most powerful). A customer can have more than one role with a
   product. Power may vary depending on the role.

7. What discoveries did you make?
   a. _____
   b. _____
   c. _____
   d. _____

EXERCISE 3: INFORMATION IS POWER

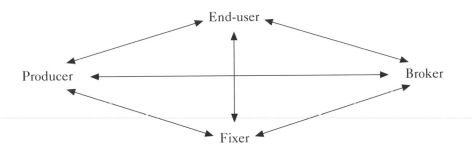

1. Circle your own role for the product named previously.

2. Prioritize the level of interaction and communication flow between the players by putting a "1" on the line between the two who interact most, a "2" on the line between the two that interact next most frequently, and so on.

3. What specific actions could help increase the intensity or quality of interaction between the end-user and producer?

_____

_____

_____

Notes

1. Karen Lowry, "Can This Hot-Rodder Make Honda Racy Again?" *Business Week*, 9 July 1990, 58–59.

2. George E. Wollner, "The Law of Producing Quality." *Quality Progress*, January 1992, 35–40.

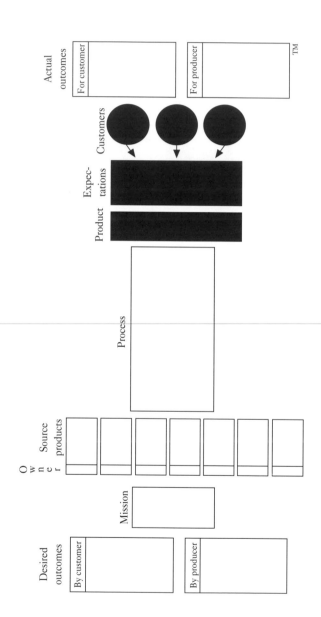

The Customer-Centered Culture Model™

Actual outcomes
For customer
For producer
TM

Customers

Expec-
tations

Product

Process

Source
products

O
w
n
e
r

Mission

Desired
outcomes
By customer
By producer

3

Defining Customer Expectations

So far, we've talked about products as any deliverables that are described as nouns, occur in countable units, can be made plural, and are created to satisfy customer expectations. We've identified three customer roles: end-users, brokers, and fixers. These roles are always determined by the specific product of interest. Although a customer primarily holds one of these roles, he/she could also have any of the other roles as well.

In an ideal world, there are only producers and end-users. The producer talks with the prospective end-user to discover needs. The product is then built to fit customer expectations exactly. As enlightened producers, we consider each individual user as a distinct, important market niche. Fixers are irrelevant since the product is right the first time and lasts indefinitely. The broker role, if any, exists to create benefits for end-users and producers without filtering the information flow between them. Believe it or not, there are a number of businesses which operate as if this ideal is the only acceptable approach to customer satisfaction.

For those of us who are not pursuing this ideal, the alternate future looks bleak. The unfortunate reality is that many enterprises use a one-size-fits-all approach to product design. Henry Ford used this as a basis for providing customers with color choices on Model Ts. If you wanted black, you were going to be happy. Otherwise, you were out of luck. Black was Ford's preference because it dried faster than other colors.

Other organizations may simply skip the product design phase in which where the producer asks prospective customers what they want. This happens often. Consider the customer revolt when Coca-Cola changed its product formulation.

As producers, we often act as if we know what customers want. But if we haven't checked recently (if ever), we are at risk. We should use caution in applying benchmarking or industry standards as the basis for determining how good we are. The potential conclusion could be that if we are doing as well as or better than our competition, we're going to meet customer expectations. We need to be careful of who's setting the standards: producers or customers. Industry standards are producer standards. They perpetuate producer-centered thinking and may not have much relationship to customer expectations. The computer industry offers an example.

IBM has long dominated the computer business. A main reason is because it does a lot of things well. Its hardware design strategy has been classically producer-centered. The "closed architecture" of IBM's computers kept customers chained to the company. Good news for IBM, bad news for customers who wanted to enable different machines to share the same software. The customer revolt that has been going on since the mid-1980s is based on customer demands for "open systems." If the past is any predictor of the future, we will again see the end-users win in the long run. Both IBM and Apple Computer will need to refocus on customer expectations. There is evidence that this is beginning to occur.

I would like to relate a personal story that illustrates a core principle for creating a customer-centered culture. When I was a kid, I loved to play in my friends' houses. My house was boring. I knew all the people there and was overly familiar with all the contents. One place that was always new and different was the house of one of my dad's friends, Charlie, who had traveled to different countries and who spoke other languages. He had numerous hobbies, including photography, astronomy, hunting, and fishing. Whenever I had a question about something, he had an answer.

One day while visiting at Charlie's house, I noticed an unusual package leaned up against the hall closet. Charlie told me it was a rifle and asked if I'd like to see it. Naturally, I said yes. He put the rifle, still in its padded case, on the sofa. Without unzipping it, he asked me if I thought it was loaded. What would you have said? I told him I didn't know. He told me that, for safety reasons, I should always assume a gun is loaded until I had checked it. This is the essential principle to be safe regarding customer needs: *Always assume customer expectations are unmet, until you've checked*.

With this frame of reference, we can determine what customers really expect. It is preferable to do this *before* we create a product. Sometimes this is done. However, the reality may be that the product you began to focus on in Chapter 1 was created without first defining customer expectations. If so, don't feel too bad: Unfortunately, this happens all the time. We'll walk through the process you can use either to verify that the product is right or modify it appropriately. An exercise near the end of the chapter will help you implement what we'll cover. This process will be most successful if we can emotionally "let go" of the present product and be prepared to redesign it completely based on defined customer expectations.

In our work with many clients, we have found that customer satisfaction is based on three major criteria:

1. *Performance* of the service or manufactured product, defined by objective criteria. The focus is on the product's function.
2. *Perception* of the product and related subjective criteria. Focus is on appeal or subjective experience.
3. *Outcome* or results obtained by using the service or manufactured product.

Customers tend to mix these three factors together when they communicate their needs. Our challenge as producers is to separate these criteria so we can appropriately design the product.

PERFORMANCE CRITERIA

Performance expectations are primarily focused on whether the product performs as wanted. If our product is a car, customers may say they want such performance attributes as "good gas mileage," "starts in cold weather," "quick acceleration," and "body doesn't rust out." These statements are called *true quality characteristics* and are made in nontechnical language by the customer. In this case, they seem to address performance. But what does "good gas mileage" really mean? Customers differ in what "good" is, indicating a perception. Certainly, the objective criterion for gas mileage is miles per gallon. This is the performance attribute to be addressed. Through discussions with our customers, we can determine that today's family sedan customers think 30 or more miles per gallon is good gas mileage. The related outcome customers want, as implied by "good gas mileage," is minimal cost to operate the car. Even customer needs which seem to be focused on performance often contain perception and outcome expectations.

The true quality characteristics of good gas mileage must be broken down into objectively measurable parts. In this case, 30 miles per gallon is an example of objective criteria. This is called a *substitute quality characteristic* (SQC). It is not exactly the same as good gas mileage, but its measurability makes it useful for design purposes. SQCs always consist of a unit of measure and a performance (objective) attribute. (We address this in greater detail in the next chapter.)

If the product is a budget report (a knowledge/service product), the managers who receive it may say they want performance attributes like "accurate numbers," "published within five days of month's end," and "includes all budget items." We can objectively determine if these expectations are met. "Accurate numbers" could be translated into a substitute quality characteristic of "zero errors" and be measured.

PERCEPTION OF THE PRODUCT

The second factor, perception, addresses appeal, product configuration, packaging, delivery, and sensory impact on the customer. In the case of the car, such attributes might be stated as "comfortable ride," "good visibility," and "stylishness." For the budget report, the recipient may ask that it is "easy to read." All these attributes are highly subjective.

Determining what "stylish" or "easy to read" means for a variety of customers is a challenge. In the next chapter we'll discuss how to measure these. For now, it's important simply to know that these subjective criteria exist in the customer's mind and we have to have a way of revealing them.

OUTCOME CRITERIA

The third factor, outcome, addresses the results achieved by use of the product. It focuses on the customer's purpose for the product. For the car, that purpose might be cheap, flexible transportation. The purpose of the budget report could include "help me decide quickly whether I can buy the new equipment." Understanding the customer's intended outcome enables us to determine whether the product is the best one for the job. Designing for outcomes is the key to providing quality that excites and delights customers.

Whereas the first two factors, performance and perception, are truly focused on the product, outcome is focused on results. Understanding outcome is the key to innovation. We'll address that topic in more detail later. For now, let's keep things simple by addressing performance and perception.

SEPARATING PERFORMANCE FROM PERCEPTION

All organizations seem to have a bias toward either performance or perception. Technically oriented functions like engineering or data processing are likely to emphasize performance criteria. A marketing organization may focus on perception attributes. No matter what bias the producing organization has, the customer's priority is what counts. An example will help make this clear. Several years ago, my wife had major knee surgery. Just before her release from the hospital, the surgeon came by to make a final check and sign the release papers. To check how the incision was healing, he removed a couple of bandage strips covering the wound. Everything seemed fine, there was no infection or abnormal swelling. He asked her to come back again in several weeks to be rechecked.

On our next visit, we had our customary 45-minute wait before the surgeon came into the examination room. The surgeon asked, "How are *we* doing today?" My wife said she could only speak for herself but that *she* was feeling fine. Then she pointed out that the incision had spread apart where the surgeon had removed the bandages, whereas the other part of the healed incision was nice and tight. The surgeon replied, "But at least you can walk now."

My wife was shocked to hear his response and tried again to convey how she felt about the appearance of the scar. The surgeon still didn't get it. After the appointment, my wife did what most dissatisfied customers do: She told everyone else about it. She would never have that surgeon work on her again. He did not understand her needs.

In this situation, the product was a joint replacement. A number of attributes were expected by my wife, the end-user. Do you think the surgeon had a bias toward performance or perception attributes? Like many technically oriented professionals, his focus was on performance ("at least you can walk"). This is something like taking your car into the garage because it has trouble starting on a cold morning. When you get the car back, it starts just fine but there's grease and grime on the upholstery. What's wrong with that picture?

Performance   *Perception*

Figure 3-1: Quality requires balance.

Customers also have biases about performance and perceptual attributes. The producer's task is to match the customer's priorities. The more robust the quality of the product, the more likely it is to be the right balance for the greatest number of customers.

Internal reports offer another great example of the importance performance and perception expectations play in customer satisfaction. Most managers receive monthly reports. Depending on the functional group the manager is in, this might be a departmental budget report, sales report, profit/loss statement, or production report. It may be several pages (or inches) thick and could look something like the example in Table 3-1. Give yourself only five seconds to look at that table. How is this company doing on sales? You may have to spend considerably longer than five seconds to answer this question.

Now give yourself only three seconds to review Figure 3-2. How is the company doing on sales? You can probably tell right away. Most people can't determine how well sales are doing by looking briefly at Table 3-1. Both reports contain the data needed to answer this question, and both have the same performance attribute of "accurate monthly volume and revenue data." The second report also provides the perceptual attribute of "trend and relationship of volume and revenue data."

Which of these two styles of report—tabular or graphic—do you receive? Which would you prefer? The vast majority of managers we've asked prefer the graphic version because it takes less time to understand and act upon (outcome). People tend to make judgments and decisions based on

Sample Sales Data Report Gross Profit by Product Line April–September, 1990						
	A	M	J	J	A	S
Unit sales	175	184	226	76	84	99	
Sales							
Product 1	4,187	7,756	983	2,371	13,704	36,386	65,387
Product 2	31,054	26,835	21,501	17,018	18,924	24,287	139,619
Product 3	2,205	0	0	3,125	550	2,425	8,305
Total sales	37,446	34,591	22,484	22,514	33,178	63,098	213,311
Cost of sales							
Product 1	1,553	-66	3,181	1,112	934	3,579	10,293
Product 2	21,176	7,073	24,457	17,113	16,052	27,980	113,851
Product 3	1,356	126	484	2,452	331	1,103	5,852
Total cost	24,085	7,133	28,122	20,677	17,317	32,662	129,996
Gross profit							
Product 1	2,634	7,822	-2,198	1,259	12,770	32,807	55,094
Product 2	9,878	19,762	-2,956	-95	2,872	-3,693	25,768
Product 3	849	-126	-484	673	219	1,322	2,453
Total GP	13,361	27,458	-5,638	1,837	15,861	30,436	83,315

Table 3-1: Tabular report.

patterns. The graphic representation of the data adds value. Graphics employ symbolic language to illustrate the truism "a picture is worth a thousand words." Some managers have said they want both tabular and graphic reports but would use the graphic display first to determine what, if any, detail to pursue in the tabular data version. Most receive only the tabular report.

When was the last time the producer of your reports asked you what you wanted? If never, you are on the receiving end of a producer-centered culture. Most managers we've asked cannot recall ever being asked how reports should be designed or packaged for them. The producers of these reports may be the data processing department or the management infor-

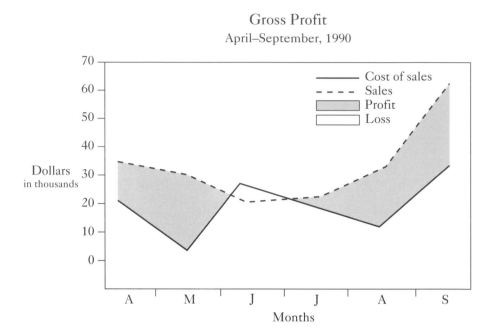

Figure 3-2: Graphic report.

mation systems (MIS) department. Some MIS managers respond, in their defense, that they can't possibly meet the individual needs of all users of all reports. Yet unless these users are asked what they want, MIS really isn't in a position to say it can't be done. There is a difference between an excuse and a reasonable justification. If we, as producers, are making decisions on what will be good for our customers without their active input, we are sustaining a producer-centered culture.

One of the excuses given for not creating many different versions of a report (and other products) is the added cost. It is true that MIS may incur more cost to provide reports in the format users want. The MIS budget would easily reveal this cost.

How about the cost the users presently incur by getting reports that need to be "fixed"? The user's budget does not capture the cost of his/her time wasted trying to find information buried in the report, modifying the report to show trends, or throwing out most of the report which is not needed. The cumulative "cost-to-use" of a poor product (across all customers) is usually much greater than the additional cost to produce the right product for the right users the first time. What is the true cost of providing unusable products? We'll address this in our discussion of Taguchi in Chapter 6.

This tendency to measure only the cost to produce, without measuring the cost to use, is a major reason our organizations are unresponsive to customers' needs. Changing this common practice is critical to transforming our culture and becoming leaders.

We've been discussing the need to balance the performance and perception attributes, based on customer priorities. When we compare customer expectations with the actual product, we almost always find that one of three types of relationships exists, as shown in Figure 3-3.

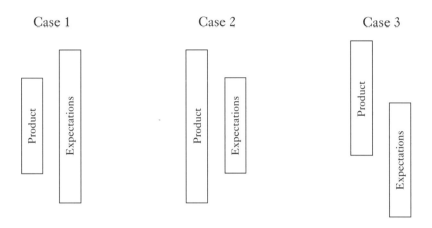

Figure 3-3: Improvement opportunities vary when expectations differ from the product.

Expectations consist of both performance and perception attributes. In case 1, the product doesn't measure up to expectations. This represents an opportunity to improve low quality. In the example of the financial report, the user wanted a graphic display of the data and got only a tabular display. The good news is that the right information was included.

Case 2 shows the product exceeding expectations. Contrary to popular opinion, this is not necessarily a good thing. If the financial report is 25 pages long, how much is actually read by the user? Our research has found that the typical manager will read less than 10 percent of the tabular report and often less than 5 percent. This situation represents an opportunity for productivity improvement. Significant amounts of time, energy, and resource are used to create a product that the customer may not need or use. The producer may be creating waste on a routine basis. Another example concerns billing statements sent to customers. The statement is a service product. We have repeatedly heard from end-users that they prefer bills be sent without additional promotional material in the envelopes. Some have mistakenly thrown away phone bills, utility bills, and credit card bills because they thought the envelope only contained junk mail. The producer's objective of using the billing process to sell more product may compete with the customer's desire.

We should not confuse the over-engineered, voluminous financial report product with products that provide more value than customers' initially expect. It's one thing to provide a product that exceeds customer expectations when the unexpected is also unwanted. It is quite another thing to provide a product that exceeds expectations on *relevant* issues and at the same time creates new wants that are satisfied. We call this leadership. In manufactured products, a classic example of this second situation is illustrated by cars. Historically, American-made cars have been offered à la carte. The buyer is quoted a price for the stripped-down vehicle. "Extras" like air conditioning and a stereo are added to the base price. The fact that most car buyers wanted these extras prompted Japanese auto manufacturers to include these components as standard equipment. True, not all customers expected the basic car to include those features. But these additions were not unwanted, and expectations have subsequently changed. A luxury, once experienced, often becomes a necessity. The Japanese also discovered that by making fewer options available, product complexity and cost were reduced. The producer needs to be careful that if the product exceeds expectations, the excess is both wanted and worth it.

The third case in Figure 3-3 shows an opportunity for improvement that has parts of both case 1 and case 2 in it. This illustrates that the product (1) meets some of the customer's expectations, (2) doesn't have some characteristics that are wanted, and (3) provides some attributes that are not wanted. It is a natural result of failure to define clearly customer segmentation or groupings.

Case 3 is reality for the typical product. The financial report probably fits this situation: The basic data is shown, but it's not shown in desired graphic display, and the report has more pages and data than are required or wanted.

It can be important to know which type of improvement opportunity exists with the product since the correction strategy may differ. In any case, we must have the necessary information on customer expectations to determine how much of a match exists with the product. Exercise 4 will help you do this. It is the prerequisite to our discussion about measurements in Chapter 4.

The customer expectations exercise should be done with a group of four to eight people. Ideally, they should include real customers of the product on which you will focus. If that is not possible, invite participation by colleagues who know something about the real end-users' likely expectations. The whole exercise will take at least 45 minutes. The results will be quite revealing.

I have been very pleased to see a large number of MIS and other functional groups quickly seek input from their customers after going through this exercise in our training. The customer-centered organization seeks out customer needs on all its products on a continuous basis and then redesigns or modifies the products accordingly.

The process used in Exercise 4 can easily be applied to any product. In essence, it is a structured focus group process. You are asked to focus on end-users because their interests should be your highest priority. The same process can and should be used with the various brokers and fixers who also have experience with the product. Attribute priorities among the three groups are likely to differ. This information can be helpful to share in discussions with representatives of those three customer groups. Those different customers' priorities may initially appear to be in competition with each other. By negotiating a consensus on the priority of the product attributes, you have the basis for modifying or redesigning the target product so it satisfies everyone. When in doubt, favor the end-user. Important note: If you do not include the real end-users in this exercise, do not proceed until you do so. As producers, we absolutely must ensure that we are not speaking for end-users. The only way to avoid a fatal result is to ask them.

This only begins the process of transferring the voice of the customer (VOC) into product design requirements. The exercise specifically asks you to focus on VOC, not on product content specifics. The "is" in the attribute guide "a quality (<u>name of product</u>) is one that *is* (<u>attribute</u>)" ensures the right answers. If you change "is" to "has," you'll end up with features, not product functions. (Changing "is" to "results in" will identify outcomes. We address this in Chapter 5.) The next step will involve identification of the features, content, or component characteristics to be incorporated into the product design.

EXERCISE 4: CUSTOMER EXPECTATIONS

	Expected time (minutes)

1. Each person in the group is responsible for recording notes. Assign a timekeeper.
2. Write the name of the target product. Remember that this product name must meet the following criteria:
   - is a noun
   - occurs in countable units
   - is specific
   - can be made plural

The name of a class of products—reports, answers, orders, plans, and so on—is not specific enough. Select the *specific* product name you will focus on. **(2)**

3. Identify all the end-users for this product and write their names in the blanks. **(3)**

4. Brainstorm by giving each participant a turn to state an attribute thought to be desired by end-users. Everyone writes down each attribute as it is stated. The objective is to *quickly* identify as many attributes as possible. The goal is 30; the minimum is 15. Limit discussion.

Important note:

Attributes must be stated in the "voice of the customer" using this statement:

A quality _(product name)_ is one that is _(attribute)_ . *Do not* change any of the words in this statement to fit your attributes.

Be careful that attributes identified are for the product named, not for some other product. If the product is a purchase order, the attributes are for the purchase order itself, not the items the purchase order represents. **(12)**

5. Once all the attributes are written down (or time runs out), each participant reviews the list to identify which three attributes are thought to be most important. Put a check in the "rank" column next to those three. This is done by each individual, without discussion. Do not combine or group attributes. *Do the remaining steps (6 through 10) through group discussion.* **(2)**

6. Determine the rank or priority of attributes by recording (in the "rank" column) the number of checks each attribute has received. The one with most checks is ranked "1." Quickly rank the top five only. No ties are allowed. Breaking the ties arbitrarily is okay. Complete steps 7 through 9 regarding only these top five attributes. **(3)**

7. Put a check in "M" column next to those attributes that are currently measured. Consider an attribute "currently measured" only if a numerical measure is published, reported, or displayed on a regular basis. **(4)**

8. Determine whether each of the top five attributes addresses performance (objective criteria) or perception (subjective criteria). Put a check in the appropriate "perf" or "perc" column. It is okay to indicate that the attribute addresses both performance and perception. **(3)**

9. Total the number of checks in the "perf" and "perc" columns. **(1)**

10. Summarize your experience by answering the following questions: **(15)**
    a. What is the target product?
    b. Who are the end-users?
    c. How many attributes were identified?
    d. What was the number 1 attribute?
       1) Is it currently being measured? How?
       2) Does the attribute address performance, perception, or both?
    e. Repeat steps 4a and 4b for attributes 2 through 5
    f. What was the hardest part of this exercise?
    g. What discoveries were made during the exercise?

Total estimated minutes	45

CUSTOMER EXPECTATIONS EXERCISE

Product _____   End-users _____
_____   _____
_____   _____

	Attributes	Rank	M	Perf	Perc
1					
2					
3					
4					
5					
6					
7					
8					
9					
10					
11					
12					
13					
14					
15					
16					
17					
18					
19					
20					
21					
22					
23					
24					
25					
26					
27					
28					
29					
30					
			Totals		

> A *quality product is one that*
> *is* = functions
> *has* = features
> *results in* = outcomes

For example, you may have identified "easy to use" as an attribute end-users want. It so happens this attribute is one of three that we have found virtually all customers (for all products) rank among the top five. Your challenge is to break "easy to use" into more detailed attributes you can design for and measure. Going back to the example of the financial report product, "easy to use" might be broken down to include the following:

- Can be understood at a glance
- Is printed on 8 1/2 x 11 paper (so it can be filed in standard notebooks)
- Shows positive numbers in one color (for example, black)
- Shows negative numbers in a different color (for example, red)
- Provides a one-page graphic summary
- Refers to the location of related details within supporting documents (either attached or elsewhere)

These increasingly detailed attributes are called substitute quality characteristics. They can be used more readily than "easy to use" for design purposes. The structured method that takes this further is called QFD, developed by Yoji Akao and first used at the Kobe shipyards in 1972. To use words which are more intuitively understandable, consider QFD to mean customer-centered design. The details are beyond the scope of this book but can be pursued through the sources listed in the Bibliography. We will examine some additional aspects in Chapter 4, since they regard measurement.

Conclusion
Your experience with the customer expectations exercise may be similar to that of our clients. Discoveries, stated in the words of participants in our workshops, include the following:

- We don't measure what customers want.
- Some management goals and measures conflict with end-user needs.

- The end-users' priorities are different from our producer interests. This difference is seen in terms of the specific attributes wanted as well as the emphasis on perception attributes over performance (or vice versa).
- It is easy to start thinking inadvertently about the final (or another) product when discussing the intermediate information product.
- There are competing needs among customers.
- It is hard to avoid thinking of features. We were tempted to use "has" instead of "is."
- If we measure anything, we only measure performance not perception.
- Using "is" kept us focused on how our customers think.
- We are stronger at measuring performance than perception.

Among the top five attributes most wanted by customers, we have consistently found the following three included: *ease of use*, *timeliness* (that is, duration of time, delivery on time, response time), and *certainty* (consistency, reliability, accuracy, and predictability). Most of the customers' priority attributes are not measured at present. Conversely, measures linked to producer interests (volume, yield, cost, profit, productivity, and schedule) *are* being collected. To the extent this situation exists, we have a producer-centered culture.

Some producers are amazed to find that customers are much more interested in perception than in performance attributes. One explanation for this is that a product's technical aspects (that is, accuracy, completeness, consistency, capability) are expected; customers expect the product to work. This means that attributes which enable a product to meet "expected quality" standards are going to have greater impact on dissatisfaction if they are not there than on satisfaction if they are there. We expect our flight to arrive on time. We don't feel especially overjoyed when it does. But we are generally dissatisfied when it is late. We may not be expecting the flight attendant to greet us by name and help us put our luggage in the overhead bin. When it happens, it is a satisfier (since this is so rare).

Since it is tough enough for producers just to get the performance attributes to work, it's even more of a challenge to address the fuzzy perception attributes. But this is an essential requirement for creating customer loyalty and excitement. It is certainly true that when we can measure something we can manage it. That is the focus of the next chapter.

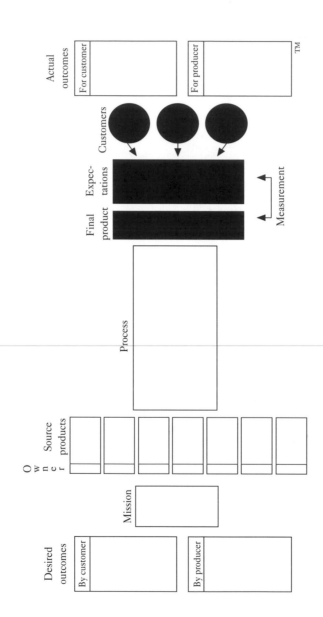

The Customer-Centered Culture Model™

4

Measuring Service Quality

The vast majority of organizations would have us believe customer satisfaction is a top priority. Maybe it is. The fact is that customer satisfaction can be a pretty fuzzy thing to measure, especially when compared with concepts measured in hard numbers, such as profit, cost, yield, and volume. Pick up the annual report of any public company and see where the customer satisfaction numbers are published. Your search is likely to have disappointing results.

Many in the quality management field would say customer satisfaction and quality are related. If customer satisfaction is the goal, then quality is the yardstick for measuring the degree to which customer expectations are achieved. Again, the typical annual report will be mute on quality numbers.

I've wondered for years why this is so. Could it be we don't know how to measure our quality? Perhaps we know but don't publish this information because we're not proud of our quality. Is this information too secret to share with investors, employees, and the financial community?

Measurement is management's way of saying "we care." Motorola is an excellent example of how to demonstrate commitment to customer satisfaction through measurement. My consulting firm began working with Motorola in 1986. The company won the Malcolm Baldrige National Quality Award in 1988. Its 1988 annual report, published prior to winning the award, was unique.

Not only was its corporate objective of total customer satisfaction addressed on page 2, but it outlined the five key initiatives being used to achieve that goal. The annual report included numerous statistics on quality improvement for a variety of corporate groups. Even the casual reader knew Motorola was not simply giving lip service to the objective of total customer satisfaction.

Measurement is management's way of saying "we care."

One of Motorola's five key initiatives in support of its objective is called "six sigma." This statistical term means that Motorola intends to have no more than 3.4 defects per million manufacturing and service products created. Practically speaking, this is perfection. To accomplish this, you have to know what customers want, measure how close you are, and then eliminate any gap between the two.

The airline industry has had great success in exceeding Motorola's six sigma quality objective in one area. An airline's core product is a flight. There is less than one crash per million flights. Good thing! However, the airlines are nowhere near this level of performance regarding delivered bags. A carrier commonly has several thousand mishandled or lost passenger bags per million shipped. Clearly, safety is of paramount importance. But if we can manage to deliver a complex product like a flight, luggage should get there, too. Both deal with two of the three attributes we discussed in the previous chapter: certainty and timeliness.

One of the difficulties with measurement is that there are so many things that could be measured. Our clients at one bank had created over 500 quality measures before we began to work with them. That number reflects a lack of priority. It reminds me of the military adage "If it moves, salute it; if it doesn't, paint it." The things we choose to measure may be influenced by our organizational function (auditors measure dollars and costs), our position (executives look at return on net assets), the basis for reward (meeting schedule or volume targets), or the cultural values of the organization.

PRODUCER V. CUSTOMER-CENTERED MEASURES

A popular saying of the 1980s was "The one who dies with the most toys wins." What we measure reveals our values and priorities. Table 4-1 summarizes issues that many of our clients have identified that reflect producer-centered and customer-centered cultural priorities.

Producer priorities	Customer priorities
• Productivity	• Ease of use
• Schedule	• Timeliness
• Standards	• Certainty
• Cost to produce	• Cost to own/use
• Volume	• Variety/choice

Table 4-1: Measurement priorities.

Which of these variables are measured by your own organization? Producer priorities seem heavily weighted by measures of organizational performance. Conversely, customer priorities are almost always determined by product performance, outcomes achieved through use of the product, and relationships with the producer.

In my experience, it is extremely rare to find an organization measuring the customer's experience with the product's ease of use, timeliness, or certainty. Of these three, the most important variable tends to be ease of use. Timeliness and certainty (accuracy, reliability, consistency, predictability) are the variables most likely to be measured, but they may only be measured from the producer's perspective, not the customer's.

DEVELOPING CUSTOMER-CENTERED MEASURES

Let's walk through two examples. The first represents the measurement challenges regarding many externally purchased services. The second example is drawn from the human resource organization of one of our clients. It represents similiar measurement issues for internally consumed knowledge/service products. The steps we will use are summarized in Table 4-2.

---

1. Identify the target product.

2. Describe the customer-desired attributes of the product.

3. Organize and label VOC attribute groups.

4. Identify possible substitute quality characteristics (SQCs).

5. Determine the relationship between VOCs and SQCs.

6. Prioritize which SQCs to address first.

7. Select the type of measures to use.

8. Determine the target value for priority SQCs.

Table 4-2: Developing customer-centered measures.

Example 1: Measurement of a Repair

Consider your experience when taking your car in for a repair. You drive 20 minutes from home to the shop. When you drop off the car at 7:30 A.M., the service representative tells you the work will probably cost $150 to 200 and require an hour of labor, and that the car will be available for pick-up anytime after 4 P.M.

After work, a colleague takes you the 15 miles back to the shop at 5:30 P.M. You pay $198 and drive your car home. If the garage (the producer) is measuring anything regarding this repair, the variables typically include:

1. Dollar value of the repair (price)
2. Cost of parts required
3. Labor time (difference between start and end time, as shown by time clock)
4. Labor cost (hourly labor rate times time)
5. Profit (for both the repair and the parts)

6. Volume of repairs per month
7. Number of returns to correct an inadequate repair.

Which of these measures addresses ease of use? Ease of use could be a lot better than it is. The producer requires the customer to make two round-trips to the garage: once to drop off the car and once to pick it up. The customer is also required to drop it off first thing in the morning and leave it for 10 hours, even though the repair only takes 1 hour. The producer is unlikely to be measuring round-trips or miles driven. If the garage provides its customers with rental cars, it probably measures rental revenue and car utilization and strives to increase them both. In this case, either we don't measure ease of use or what we do measure (also called incentives) encourages us to do more of the wrong thing from the customer's perspective.

Which of these measures address timeliness from the customer's perspective? Waiting time and driving time are issues of concern to the customer. The producer is not measuring them. The producer may feel very pleased that the time to repair is less than the industry standard. Yet, in this example, this performance has no impact on the customer's experience of timeliness.

In the customer's view, certainty might concern the ability to predict when the car would be worked on. If we knew in advance that the car could be worked on from 7:30 to 8:30 A.M., we could bring it in and wait the hour. In our example, the producer told us only that they would get to it "as soon as possible." The producer could easily have asked when we want it to be worked on and when we needed it completed. Variation from those times can be measured.

These points are logical and easy to address. But they are seldom followed for most major service products produced by an organization. We've worked through a simple example. Let's examine methods of consistently measuring customer needs in a way that will encourage desired actions (see Figure 4-1).

Let's continue the car repair analogy. Suppose we own a repair shop. Repairs are our product. From interaction with customers, we know they always want "good service." Our customers are like customers everywhere; they convey their expectations in nontechnical language. Our challenge is to translate the VOC into more precise language which enables us to achieve what the customer wants and to measure how well we've done it.

As stated, this customer expectation is subjective. What does "good service" mean? What elements will contribute to it? This statement is

1. Identify the target product. Make this as specific as possible.
2. Describe the customer-desired attributes of the product as stated in the voice of the customer (VOC). VOC attribute statements are often expressed in subjective terms. They complete the statement "A quality product is one that is _____ ."

Examples related to service or information products include:

- easy to use
- easy to understand
- friendly
- timely
- fast
- complete
- relevant
- succinct
- organized
- accurate
- consistent
- predictable
- flexible

Examples related to manufactured products include:

- easy to use
- timely
- durable
- reliable
- complete
- stylish
- inexpensive to own
- quiet
- consistent
- customizable
- defect-free
- maintainable

3. Organize and label VOC attributes into groups, based on something they share. Examples of attribute groupings include:

- ease of use
- timeliness
- certainty

- completeness
- relevance
- affordability

4. Identify possible substitute quality characteristics (SQCs) which may be related to each VOC statement. An SQC is always expressed in two parts: the objective criteria and its unit of measure.
5. Determine the relationship between VOCs and SQCs.
6. Prioritize which SQCs to address first.
7. Select the type of measure to use for each SQC.
8. Determine what the target value should be for each priority SQC.

Figure 4-1: The measurement process.

much too fuzzy to present a clear course of action. In previous efforts to address our repair customers, we used conventional customer response cards. We asked questions like "How satisfied were you with our service?" We gave them the usual choices ranging from "very satisfied" to "very dissatisfied." The problem is, we were never able to direct specific actions as a result of this feedback. When they've been overwhelmingly satisfied, we were never quite sure what we were doing right so we could do more of it. Those surveys have been a waste of time and money in terms of helping us to direct improvement actions. We vow that this time will be different.

Step 1: Identify the Target Product

The first step is to figure out what product "good service" could apply to. Our products include the following:

- Alignments
- Tune-ups
- Transmission repairs
- Brake replacements
- Exhaust system installations
- Electrical repairs

Transmission repairs are a big revenue contributor. We've also seen a gradual decline in this business. Maybe we can increase the demand for this service product by improving "good service." We choose transmission repairs as the product to focus on. As we think about it, we begin to realize that the transmission repair, like every other repair, actually consists of a chain of service products (see Table 4-3). Some occur before the repair. They include the appointment, the order (written up when the car is dropped off), and retrievals of parts from inventory. Service products are also created after the repair. They include the shop order (written by the

---

- Appointment

- Order

- Retrieval of parts from inventory

- Transmission repair

- Shop order

- Invoice

- Directions on where to find car in lot

Table 4-3: The chain of products for transmission repair.

mechanic to describe the work done), the invoice, and the directions given the customer to find his/her car in our parking lot. Counting the actual repair, there are seven products. "Good service" could apply to all of them.

We decide to consider all these elements together as the transmission repair. Later on, we can address each of the components in more detail.

Step 2: Describe Customer-Desired Attributes of the Product

The second step in figuring out what "good service" means, relative to transmission repair, is to consider other statements customers make about good service. They often complete the statement "A quality transmission repair is one that is _____ ," filling in the blank with one of the following:

- Available quickly
- Completed fast
- Diagnosed accurately
- Predictable in cost
- Fixed right the first time
- Understandable
- Not an interruption to my mobility
- Inexpensive
- Explained completely
- Explained in a friendly manner

We discover we are not measuring any of these things either. Virtually all of them are subjective perceptions. On one hand, it can be frustrating to come up with more things we don't measure. But the good part is that we've gotten somewhat more detail about what customers consider part of a quality transmission repair. We have also gotten to the point where we can put some of these VOC statements into separate groups.

Step 3: Organize and Label VOC Attribute Groups

The third step is to group these statements and then label the groupings. We've already discovered that virtually all customers for all products want at least three attributes: ease of use, timeliness, and certainty. These attribute groups can be applied to VOC statements we addressed in step 2 (see Table 4-4).

Product attribute groups	VOC
Timeliness	Available quickly Completed fast Not a mobility interruption
Ease of use	Explained completely Explained in friendly way Understandable
Certainty	Diagnosed accurately Fixed right the first time Predictable in cost Inexpensive

Table 4-4: The organization and labeling of VOC attributes.

Step 4: Identify Possible Substitute Quality Characteristics

Organizing the attributes starts to reveal how we can go further. The fourth step is to translate VOC attributes into precise, measurable product characteristics we can design for and manage. These are called substitute quality characteristics (SQCs).

Why are they referred to as "substitutes"? VOCs are almost always subjective statements about the product. "Easy to understand" is a typical VOC. It is a perception that is impossible to measure directly. If something can be easy to understand for one person but hard to understand for another, we have to find some objective substitutes. These substitutes always have a clear relationship to the VOC. Each SQC consists of a unit of measure and an objective performance attribute.

QUESTIONS TO CREATE PERFORMANCE ATTRIBUTES OF SQCS

One technique for creating the performance attribute part of the SQCs is to finish creating the following questions related to VOC statements about the repair:

- How long…?
- How many…?
- How often…?
- How much…?

These questions address duration, quantity, frequency, and amount, respectively. Table 4-5 shows questions that could address each of the three VOC categories shown later in Table 4-7.

Every one of the questions in Table 4-5 has helped us get much closer to identifying measurable aspects of the service product "transmission repair" that the customer cares about. We'll finish the SQC definition process by attaching a unit of measure to each of these questions we want to use. For example, if "completed fast" is the focus of one or more SQCs, we will need to do two things: First, identify which of the questions are related to "completed fast," and second, consider what the appropriate unit of measure should be (minutes, hours, or days). Table 4-6 illustrates the resulting SQCs for "completed fast."

Step 5: Determine the Relationship Between VOCs and SQCs

Even though Table 4-6 shows only seven SQCs, we could easily identify over 20 to consider. Ultimately we will need to figure out which of them is most important to pursue. The process is easy:

1. Hypothesize the nature of the relationship between an SQC and all VOC statements. The choices are plus (+), minus (–), and zero (0). Use SQC 2 as an example. As the "number of days from appointment call to car being picked up" goes up, what is the expected impact on the customer's perception of "completed fast"? The relationship is inverse. We can put a minus (–) in the box shared by this SQC and VOC to show that as one goes up, the other goes down. A plus (+) indicates that as the SQC goes up, we expect the VOC to go up. A zero (0) indicates that either there is no relationship between the SQC

Possible questions to create SQCs	Timeliness	Ease of use	Certainty
How long…			
• does it take to arrange the appointment?	X	X	
• does it take from the customer's first call to pickup of repaired car?	X	X	
• does the repair last?			X
• do customers wait?	X	X	
How many…			
• times do customers ask for explanations?		X	X
• repairs are completed by the time promised?	X		X
• hours are customers without the use of their cars?	X	X	
• customers ask for their cars to be fixed while they wait?		X	
• customers ask questions about the work done on the vehicle?			X
How often…			
• do customers get the first appointment they request?	X	X	X
• do customers bring the vehicle back after repair for rework?		X	X
• does the final cost exceed the quoted cost?			X
• is the customer's name used in interaction with him/her?		X	
• do customers challenge the necessity or cost of work?			X
How much…			
• variation in cost is there from the quote?			X
• of the total customer wait time is consumed by the repair?	X		
• of the total customer wait time is comsumed by non–value-adding time?	X		

Table 4-5

and VOC or that the relationship is inconsistent across different situations.

2. Add up all the pluses and minuses in each column. For our purposes, it is not important whether the relationships are positive or negative. We only care that an SQC has a relationship with the customer's need.

Quality table

Product _____ Transmission repairs _____

Product attribute groups	Voice of the customer	Substitute quality characteristics						
		1. Percent of first appointment requests accepted by service department	2. Number of days from appointment call to car being picked up	3. Number of minutes customer is waiting	4. Number of hours vehicle is unavailable to customer	5. Number of employees required to answer a question	6. Percent of returns for additional fixing	7. Percent of dollars actual cost deviated from estimate
Timeliness	Available quickly							
	Completed fast							
	Not an interruption to mobility							
Ease of use	Explained completely							
	Understandable							
	Explained in friendly way							
Certainty	Diagnosed accurately							
	Fixed right the first time							
	Predictable in cost							
	Inexpensive							
	Priority							
	Target value							

Table 4-6

Quality table

Product _____ Transmission repairs

Product attribute groups	Voice of the customer	1. Percent of first appointment requests accepted by service department	2. Number of days from appointment call to car being picked up	3. Number of minutes customer is waiting	4. Number of hours vehicle is unavailable to customer	5. Number of employees required to answer a question	6. Percent of returns for additional fixing	7. Percent of dollars actual cost deviated from estimate
Timeliness	Available quickly	+	—	—	—	—	—	○
	Completed fast	+	—	—	—	—	—	○
	Not an interruption to mobility	+	—	—	—	○	—	○
Ease of use	Explained completely	○	○	○	○	—		
	Understandable	○	○	○	○	—		
	Explained in friendly way	○	○	○	○	○		
Certainty	Diagnosed accurately	○	+	—	—	—	—	—
	Fixed right the first time	○	○	—	○	○	○	○
	Predictable in cost	○	○	+	○	○	—	—
	Inexpensive	○	○	—	—	○	—	○
	Priority	3	4	7	6	5	9	5
	Target value							

Substitute quality characteristics

Table 4-7

Step 6: Prioritize Which SQCs to Address First

Life is short. It can be inappropriate, if not impossible, to design for all SQCs at once. Our objective is to work on the critical few that will have the greatest impact on customer satisfaction. This step aims to select the SQC with the greatest priority (highest number of pluses *and* minuses) to focus on first. The example in Table 4-7 shows the results of our efforts in steps 5 and 6. SQCs 6, 3, and 4, in that order, have highest priority.

Step 7: Select the Types of Measures to Use

The seventh step is to consider what kinds of measures to develop. There are four: nominal, ordinal, variability, and relationship. *Nominal* measures are used when we divide things into categories (men and women; fast and slow; good and bad; small, medium, and large; and so on). Nominal measures are the least sophisticated type of measure. In our example, we could divide repairs into types: engine, transmission, electrical, front end, or brakes (see Figure 4-2). Counts and ratios are nominal measures. The numbers of repairs in each category are counted.

Ordinal measures reflect priority, sequence, rank, or rating. An ordinal measure could show the relative demand for different types of repairs. In Figure 4-3, brakes rank first in demand. In Figures 4-4 and 4-5 we see that transmissions rank first in both revenue and complaints.

These charts use both nominal (categories) and ordinal (rank) measures. Survey questions that ask the respondent to rank satisfaction on a five-point scale also use an ordinal measure.

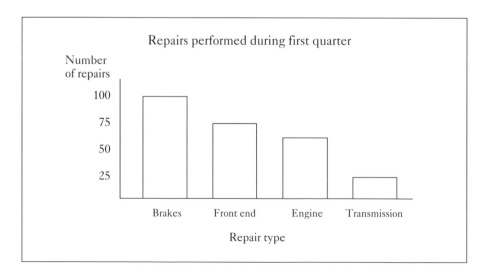

Figure 4-2: Examples of nominal measures.

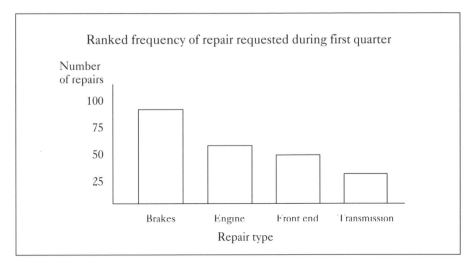

Figure 4-3: Examples of ordinal measures.

We have repeatedly found that what is measured influences (and is influenced by) what management will focus on. The most celebrated instance of this phenomenon is known as the Hawthorne effect. Western Electric discovered that workers at its Hawthorne facility improved their productivity when they knew it was being studied. The mere fact that the factory brightness/productivity ratio was being measured had an impact on worker performance. For those of us who seek to change organizational behavior, measurement can be a highly effective lever.

The rankings in Figures 4-3 and 4-4 measure producer concerns. By themselves, they might have no impact on the garage's action to address customer needs. The example in Figure 4-5 adds a whole new dimension to the meaning of the preceding two figures. Most of the complaints are about transmission repairs. This could explain why so few people ask for that type of repair. On the other hand, if transmission repairs have a greater level of profitability than other service products, our car repair business risks losing its major revenue and profit generator. Figure 4-5 should make us aware of this risk and motivate us to explore the nature and rate (over time) of the complaints.

Measures of *variability* could assist us. These may include measures of range (the difference between the highest and lowest value of a series of observations) and distribution of frequency with which an event or observation occurs. Measures of variability can be more complex than nominal and ordinal measures and can yield more information on which to

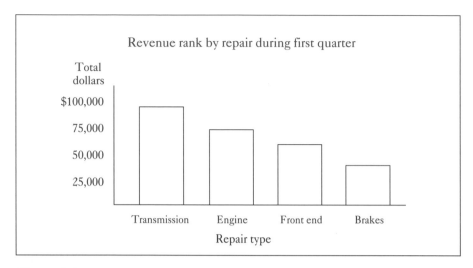

Figure 4-4

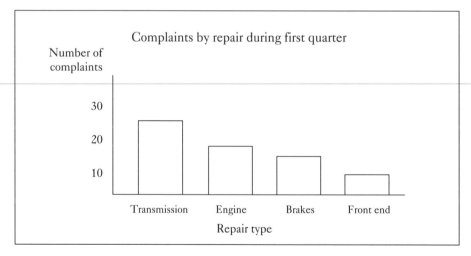

Figure 4-5

base decisions. For example, we could find that the average time from customer request for appointment to completion of the repair is nine days. Figure 4-6 shows the frequency distributions of repair times for different repairs. All average nine days.

These measures of variation help us improve our problem-solving activity and decisions. Segment B shows a normal distribution; there are an equal number of observations on either side of the most frequent

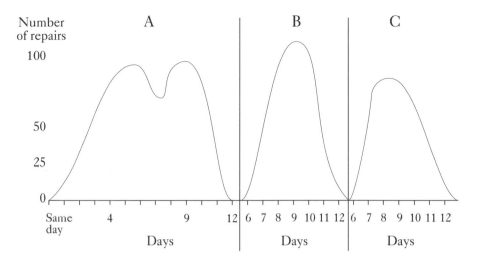

Figure 4-6: A, B, and C distribution charts.

observation (called the mode). Segment A describes two different distributions. Segment C is skewed by a few extreme observations.

The fourth type of measure concerns the *relationship* between variables. The simplest form of relationship is expressed as a ratio. One example is the percent of repairs exceeding the quoted cost. (A ratio can be a nominal measure, too.) Correlation is also a measure of relationships. The scatter diagram in Figure 4-7 shows the relationship between vehicle age and repair costs. Each dash represents one car of a given age and its repair expense at that age.

Measures of variability and relationship provide greater certainty about the meaning of a number or group of numbers. Perhaps the ultimate level of certainty is provided by a measures of prediction, a type of relationship measure which relates cause and effect. It is beyond the scope of this chapter.

The usefulness of a perception measure increases to the degree to which it is explained by a performance measure.

This discussion about types of measures is offered simply to provide awareness of alternatives. This is an extensive topic. For our purposes, it is useful to know that measures of variability and relationship generally offer much greater information than nominal and ordinal measures. If we are

Repair cost
per year

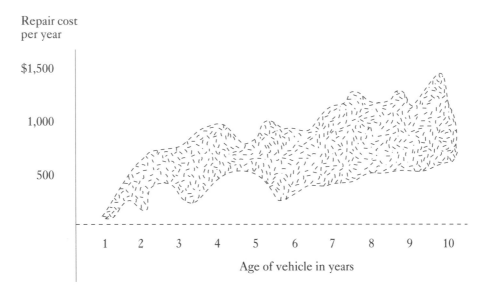

Figure 4-7: Relationship between vehicle age and repair costs.

using measurement to uncover better ways to meet customer needs and improve performance, we'll do as well as our measurements allow. The formulation of our questions of "how long," "how many," and so on was designed to give us measures of greater value than simple yes/no questions.

Step 8: Determine the Target Value for Priority SQCs

Our eighth step in the measurement process is to set numerical goals. These cannot simply be pulled from the air. Either they should be attainable under the present system or there must be clear intent to change the system so the goal will be obtained. Exhortation is not the answer.

In our example, we found that customers want repairs that are "completed fast." We have discovered through internal data collection that the average time from the customer's first call for an appointment to the time the repaired car is picked up is nine days. The distribution of these times is shown in Figure 4-8.

We also discovered that our two major competitors require their customers to wait eight to twelve days. We figure we could differentiate our service, and perhaps create a competitive advantage, by shortening the waiting time. There are at least two things we must do. First, we must decide how much differentiation we want. Could we cut the time in half?

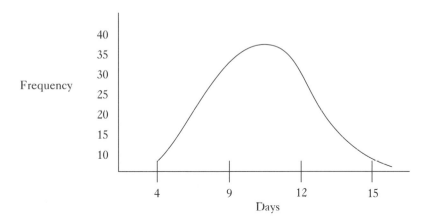

Figure 4-8: Distribution of time from the customer's first call and car pickup.

What do customers want? What costs and benefits would be associated with a change? Second, we've got to determine the causes of our present performance.

By talking with our customers, we find out they want the total time, from initial need to completed repair, to be less than seven days. Half say they would pay 10 percent extra to have the repair completed three days after the first call. We decide to pursue system changes to achieve an average of four days repair time, with 85 percent of transmission repairs occurring within two to seven days. The objectives are added to our quality table (see Table 4-8, SQC number 2).

Our intent is to change the position and shape of the distribution we currently experience. It should look like the chart in Figure 4-9.

It becomes clear that we cannot achieve our objectives by making only minor changes. After much discussion with our service employees, we decide to add an evening shift when needed. The whole process, from determining customer needs through creating the repair bill, must be redesigned. The strategies to consider are addressed in Chapter 6. Some of the seven products created in this process could be combined or redesigned.

Example 2: Measurement of a Human Resources Product

One of our clients was intrigued with the idea that a structured approach could be applied to designing a service product in the "soft" part of a business. Motivation to apply the Customer-Centered Culture

Quality table

Product _____ Transmission repairs

Product attribute groups	Voice of the customer	1. Percent of first appointment requests accepted by service department	2. Number of days from appointment call to car being picked up	3. Number of minutes customer is waiting	4. Number of hours vehicle is unavailable to customer	5. Number of employees required to answer a question	6. Percent of returns for additional fixing	7. Percent of dollars actual cost deviated from estimate
Timeliness	Available quickly	+	—	—	—	—	—	O
	Completed fast	+	—	—	—	—	—	O
	Not an interruption to mobility	+	—	—	—	O	—	O
Ease of use	Explained completely	O	O	O	O	—	—	—
	Understandable	O	O	O	O	—	O	—
	Explained in friendly way	O	O	O	O	O	—	—
Certainty	Diagnosed accurately	O	+	—	—	—	—	—
	Fixed right the first time	O	O	—	—	O	—	O
	Predictable in cost	O	O	+	O	O	—	—
	Inexpensive	O	O	—	—	O	O	O
	Priority	3	4	7	6	5	9	5
	Target value	≥90	≤4	≤60	≤96	1	0	≤10

Substitute quality characteristics

Table 4-8

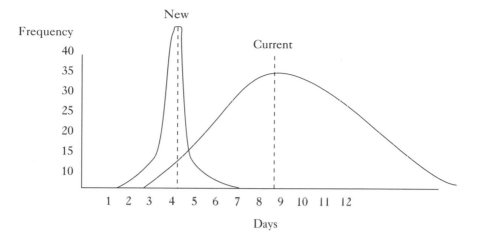

Figure 4-9: Response time.

Model™ to the human resources division of a 45,000-employee company was spurred by a class action discrimination suit. The plaintiff's successful litigation resulted in an Equal Employment Opportunity consent decree requiring the company to create a discrimination-free hiring process.

Step 1: Identify the Target Product

A team was established to address this issue. To comply with the decree, the company needed to develop an applicant tracking system. This was the product the team initially focused on. The team quickly discovered that the entire management-hiring process needed to be redesigned before an applicant tracking system could be created. But management hiring for a 45,000-person company is not just one process. The scope of such a project had to be narrowed down to something the team could get a handle on. The focus settled on the hiring process for filling management positions in the information systems (IS) division. The name of the group became the hiring process requirement (HPR) team. The team's mission: to design the optimal process for filling IS management vacancies, which meets customer needs. The target product was a competent employee in an IS management position.

Step 2: Describe the Customer-Desired Attributes of the Product

As we have seen, one of the distinguishing features of the Customer-Centered Culture Model™ is that it does not classify customers in the conventional categories of internal and external, arranged by location. Human resources' customers are predominately internal, so this simple dichotomy is of little practical value. Customers must be differentiated according to the three major roles they play regarding a specific product: end-users, brokers, and fixers.

This approach to customer differentiation was significant in helping the HPR team achieve one of its early breakthroughs. Stuck on the old paradigm, the team initially identified the hiring manager as the "customer" of the new manager. The end-users/brokers/fixers customer trichotomy helped the team realize that the new manager's subordinates were among the most important customers. This breakthrough led to interviewing employees about their expectations of a manager, which provided a brand new and worthwhile experience.

Since the design of the product (a competent person in an IS management position) required understanding customer needs, the team had to identify just who those customers were. Table 4-9 shows the customers and their roles.

The HPR team conducted several focus group discussions with the customers shown in Table 4-9. The approach for identifying customer needs was quite structured. The first step was to identify attributes that customers desired. This process was aided by having customers complete a simple sentence: A competent IS manager is one who is (attribute) . Responses included *persuasive, encouraging, effective in communication, organized, and future-oriented*.

Step 3: Organize and Label VOC Attribute Groups

Next, these customer expectations were organized into three categories: communication skills, technical skills, and problem analysis/decision-making skills. All these competencies were identified and described by customers and then validated by incumbents in the position. The list of over 33 requirements created a foundation for establishing consistency in the selection process, which would be designed later in the project.

Steps 4 Through 7: Identify Possible SQCs, Determine Relationships, Prioritize, and Select Measures

The next step in uncovering and organizing customer needs involved creating SQCs. Customer expectations that a new manager be "persuasive" and "organized" cannot be measured directly. Those statements are subjective perceptions. The development of SQCs was necessary to quantify

Product: A competent employee in an IS management position	
Customer roles	Customers
End-users	IS hiring manager Subordinates of new manager Co-workers of new manager User organization
Brokers	EEO department IS hiring manager Executive management Financial department
Fixers	Training department

Table 4-9: Customers and their roles.

candidate's qualifications objectively. An SQC consists of a unit of measure and an objective performance attribute. For example, "future-oriented" was translated into an SQC by measuring the number of project or program leadership positions the candidate had held in the past three years. Over 60 SQCs were developed. Of these, about 25 percent were found to have the highest priority and to be the most valid indicators of a quality candidate. The matrix given in Figure 4-10 provides an example. In this case, the table does not show pluses, minuses, and zeros as we have talked about. The team conducted several focus groups to identify which SQCs were perceived by different customers and the HPR team to be most important. Figure 4-10 shows the team's findings.

Even before the HPR team had concluded the project, these findings were incorporated into the hiring practices of the interviewers. A separate project was spun off to develop a new interview training curriculum that was soon implemented.

Conclusions and Exercise

We began this chapter by comparing what we are presently measuring from our producer's viewpoint with what customers care about. Our

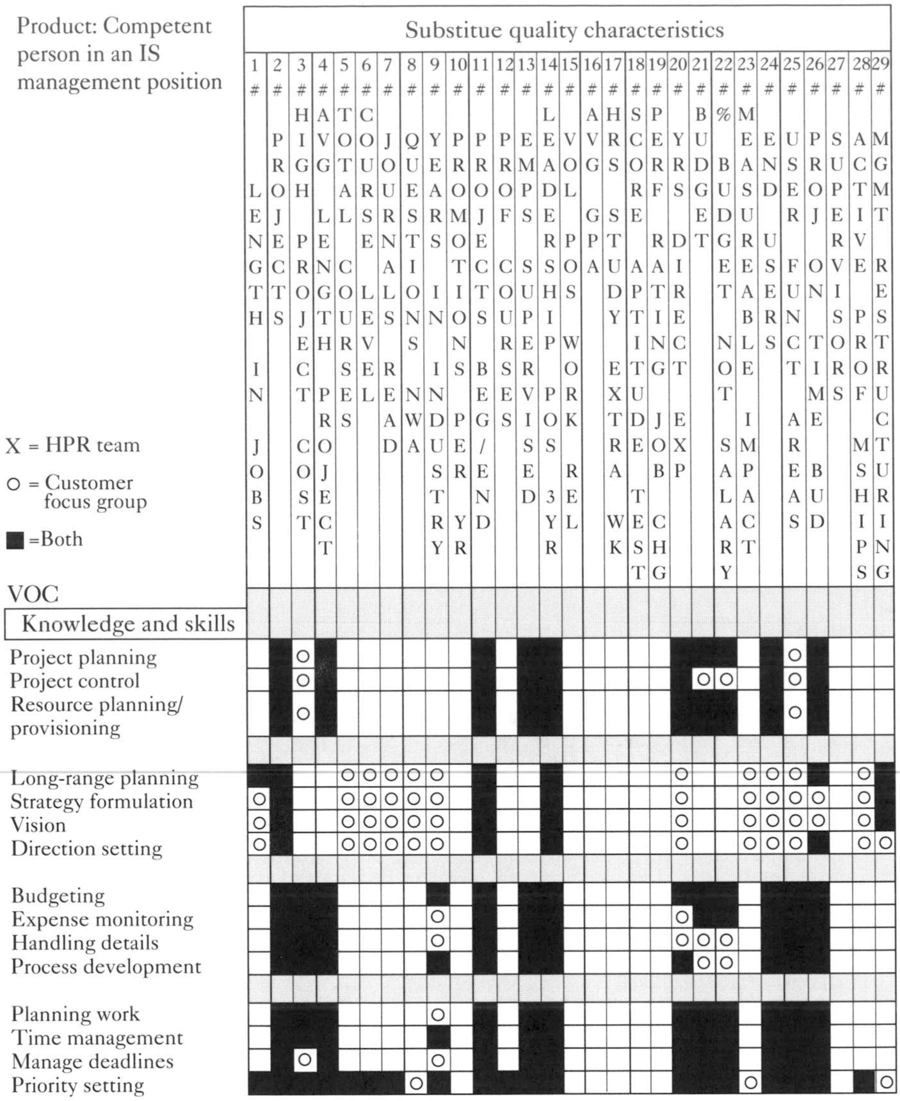
Product: Competent person in an IS management position
Substitue quality characteristics
X = HPR team
○ = Customer focus group
■ =Both
VOC
Knowledge and skills
Project planning
Project control
Resource planning/ provisioning
Long-range planning
Strategy formulation
Vision
Direction setting
Budgeting
Expense monitoring
Handling details
Process development
Planning work
Time management
Manage deadlines
Priority setting

Figure 4-10: The organization and labeling of VOC attributes.

intent has been to answer the key question "What do they want?" and make sure our measures reflect emphasis on those wants. There is a cost to improving our customers' satisfaction, but there is a larger cost not to do so.

We've worked through a process for translating perceptions, typically reflected in VOC statements, into performance measures: substitute quality characteristics. The greater the degree to which objective performance measures explain perception, the more effectively we can direct improvements. If we have implemented a change, we should be able to measure its impact. SQCs are tools to enable this.

Please complete Exercise 5, focusing on your own key product. You can do it by yourself, but it is more productive and enjoyable to work with colleagues. It will also be more accurate if you involve your end-user customers. Others have made the following discoveries.

- Many SQCs are interrelated and can influence several customer demands (VOCs).
- Defining SQCs requires a lot of dialogue and consensus.
- This process makes priority setting objective, not subjective.
- The exercise improved our team members' communication with each other.
- Almost every time we found that many "no relationship" conditions existed between one SQC and all VOCs, it was because we hadn't defined the SQC well enough.
- The highest priority SQC told us exactly what we need to do to prevent problems we've had for a long time.
- It will take effort to collect the needed measures.
- SQCs sometimes are time-related.
- The positive and negative relationships are treated as equal.
- One of the most important SQCs was "number of calls for help." This told us (1) that we must find out what is causing these calls for assistance, and (2) what features we have to consider in our product usage manual.

Notes

1. Peter M. Senge, "The Leader's New Work: Building Learning Organizations," *Sloan Management Review*, Fall 1990, 7–23.

EXERCISE 5: DEVELOPING QUALITY MEASURES FOR CUSTOMER-CENTERED DESIGN

Key principle:
> The value of a perception measure increases to the degree it is explained by a performance measure.

Instructions:
1. Name the specific target product.

2. Identify the customers on which you will focus.

3. List the voice of the customer (VOC) statements (product attributes) as stated by customers. Remember: Product attributes must fit the sentence "A quality (product) is one that is _____ ."

4. Organize and label attribute groups (that is, ease of use, timeliness, certainty, relevance, and so on).

5. Rank the VOC statements, using the multivoting technique, in order of importance to the customer. (This is described in steps 5 and 6 of Exercise 4.)

6. Identify possible substitute quality characteristics (SCQs) that may be related to each VOC statement. An SQC always consists of two parts: a unit of measure and a performance attribute (objective criteria). Use these questions to guide your brainstorming of SQCs:
   - How much _____ ?
   - How many _____ ?
   - How often _____ ?
   - How long _____ ?

   For example, if the product were an instruction booklet, one VOC attribute might be "quick to read." A related SQC "number of pages" answers the question "How many ____?" "Number of minutes to read" answers "How long _____ ?" Create a larger matrix as necessary.

7. Determine the relationship between each SQC and each VOC (+, –, or 0) and record it. A "+" indicates a direct relationship between a VOC and SQC is expected; "–" indicates an inverse relationship; "0" says there is either no expected relationship or the relationship is not consistent across all situations.

8. Total and record the number of +'s and –'s in each column. The higher the number, the more relevant and valuable the SQC is. Prioritize which SQCs to address first.

9. Decide what the target value should be for each SQC. Consider the target value from the *customer's point of view*. (For instance, how long would a customer say it should take to read an instruction booklet?)

10. Select the type of measure (nominal, ordinal, variation, relationship) and data collection technique to use for each SQC.

Quality table

① Product _____

② End users _____

④ Product attribute groups

③ Voice of the customer

⑤ Rank

⑥ Substitute quality characteristics

⑦

⑧ Priority

⑨ Target value

Ease of use

Timeliness

Certainty

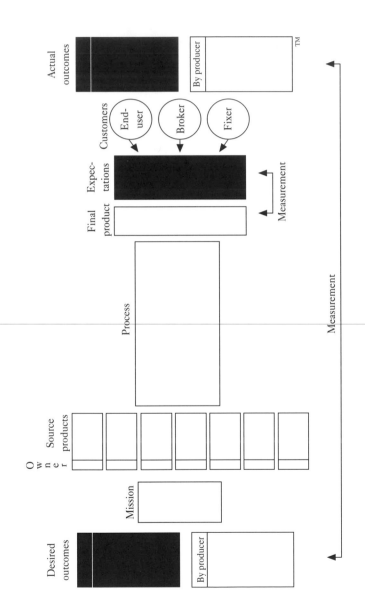

The Customer-Centered Culture Model™

5

Quality
and Innovation

What the customer buys and considers value is never a product. It is always…what a product or service does *for him.**

Peter F. Drucker

If we always do what we always did, we will always get what we always got.

Courtesy of Carl Cooper, Motorola

CONVERGENT V. DIVERGENT THINKING

The way we think about quality has changed over the years. Who is responsible for quality, how we achieve it, and what quality means are all being redefined.

In the early 1980s, when I asked top managers how they were addressing quality, they often responded, "Our quality department handles

*Exerpt from *Management: Tasks, Responsibilities, Practices* by Peter Drucker. Copyright ©1973, 1974 by Peter F. Drucker. Reprinted by permission of HarperCollins Publishers.

that." Fortunately, more managers now recognize that responsibility for quality does not reside in just one department. Every employee shares this responsibility, with management required to take the lead. As responsibility is being distributed, so must be the authority to bring about improvement. The many efforts to create participatory work styles, flatten hierarchical structures, foster employee ownership, and empower people are accelerating the distribution of authority. This change in thinking about who is responsible for quality is critical to sustaining organizational success.

One of W. Edwards Deming's major contributions has been to address how quality should be achieved. He has repeatedly made the point that quality should be obtained by examining how the manufactured or service product is put together, not through inspection and rework after the fact. One of my client businesses offers a wonderful example of what Deming is talking about.

The client business is in graphic arts. Images are its products. These images may appear as pages in a catalog, on a cereal box cover, or as ads in publications. Early in our work together, I asked the client's staff what "quality" meant to them. They couldn't define it but said it meant "doing the job right." When I asked how good their quality was, they said their customers were very happy (that is, customers weren't complaining). When I asked for supporting measures, I was told that "only" 20 percent of the jobs (orders) had to be reworked. They had a financial tracking system indicating which jobs customers rejected. These had to be redone at my client's expense. Therefore, only 80 percent of the graphic artist's work was paid for by their customers. Figure 5-1 shows their initial understanding of quality.

In essence, any job customers paid for was deemed a quality job. Through more discussion, we arrived at a quality objective:

> The [company X] quality objective is to understand our customers' needs and deliver every product on time and error-free the first time.

An "error" was defined as any work that was not initially requested by the customer. Not only did this put significant emphasis on understanding a customer's needs (not previously done in any organized way), but it revealed information about quality, as illustrated in Figure 5-2.

Figure 5-2 shows a classic case of failure to build quality into the initial product. It was inspected and reworked into acceptable condition. Those extra costs were charged to the customer. This new picture reveals

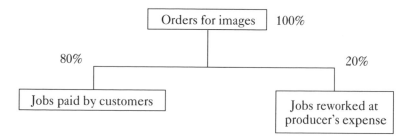

Figure 5-1: Initial understanding of quality.

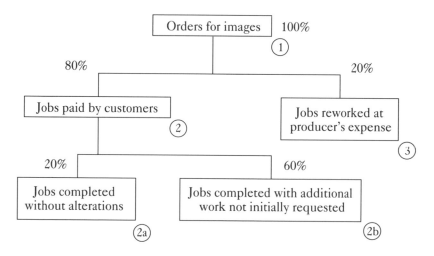

Figure 5-2: Reexamined understanding of quality.

that only 20 percent of the jobs (box 2a) were correct on the first attempt. Fully 80 percent of the work was being redone, even though the customer paid for it (boxes 2b and 3).

This example also illustrates the power of the *vital lie*, a term coined by the playwright Henrik Ibsen. It refers to things we tell ourselves to avoid questioning the truth (and thereby avoid making change). My clients' vital lie was that 80 percent of their work was to an acceptable quality level. The reality was that their initial definition (or lack of one) and measurement of quality hid from them the truth: Only 20 percent of work was done right the first time. How quality is defined is vitally important, since that is the target we'll work to hit.

The short answer to how we can build quality in is to design it in. This refers to the design of both the product and the process. Deming's focus is primarily on process—the "how" of building in quality. We'll examine process issues at greater length in our next chapter. Our focus so far has been on product design. We need to stick with this a little longer.

Managing processes to achieve quality is one of the significant changes now sweeping American business. There are at least two reasons why there is potential danger in overemphasizing process. First, process issues tend to be largely producer concerns. It is true that the customer will ultimately experience the results of process problems (via a poor-quality product), but the immediate process concerns affect the producer. Second, inordinate focus on process often coincides with an assumption that the product itself is basically sound in design. This may be a vital lie. It can also foster a minimalist approach to product change. Programs addressing "continuous improvement" are sometimes the cloaks covering this approach. This may not always be the case but, regrettably, often is.

The conventional wisdom in the United States, as promoted by Philip Crosby and others, is that quality means conformance to requirements. While this is one way of defining quality, it implies that "requirements" equal customer expectations and variation from those requirements is to be minimized. The reality is that requirements are often producer-specified and may have only a partial relationship to customer desires. In Chapters 3 and 4, we considered that few producers have measurements regarding ease of use, timeliness, and certainty as customers experience them. Are producers conforming to these customer requirements? The bottom line is that conventional wisdom tends to foster convergent thinking about quality.

Convergent thinking refers to the incremental modifications we make for improvement. Convergent thinking about quality is always product- or process-focused. In the short term, convergent thinking works well. In the long term, it spells disaster if we don't focus on the results the customer is trying to achieve by using the product. We can call these results outcomes.

One well-known example of convergent thinking was demonstrated by the railroads early in this century. They viewed themselves as being in the railroad business (product-focused), not the transportation business (outcome-focused). As a result, the new products (automobiles and airplanes) created to address transportation needs did not spring from the rail-

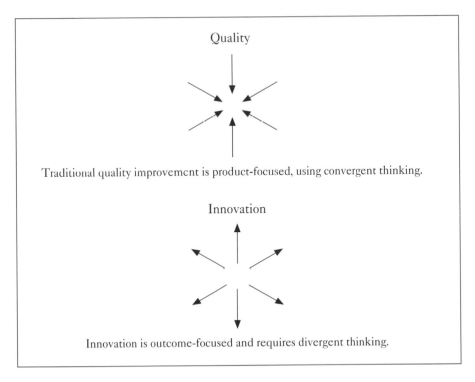

Quality

Traditional quality improvement is product-focused, using convergent thinking.

Innovation

Innovation is outcome-focused and requires divergent thinking.

Figure 5-3

road companies. The railroads lost their leadership in transportation, along with their market share.

This scenario has repeated itself countless times. As Spaniard George Santayana said long ago, "Those who cannot remember the past are sure to repeat it." Futurist Joel Barker talks about paradigms—models we have of the world. Paradigms can prevent or enable change. Today's prevailing paradigm about quality is that incremental improvement will enable organizations to remain competitive. While continuous improvement is both necessary and helpful, convergent thinking is hardly adequate to maintain or achieve leadership. If we truly want to excel, we must master the innovative process.

Innovation refers to the process of making a desired outcome easier to achieve. This process can occur in two ways. The first (and most celebrated) instance occurs unexpectedly and results in a happy coincidence. We call this serendipity. A classic example occurred recently as the University of Minnesota was developing a device to destroy toxic PCBs. During experimentation, the PCBs were successfully destroyed *and* were converted into industrial grade diamonds! The second situation occurs by design. Both processes benefit from divergent thinking.

The innovation process results in (1) creating something new, and/or (2) changing the way something is used.

Innovation requires divergent thinking, which is outcome-focused. A few examples can illustrate the size of the opportunity.

Change in product

		YES	NO
	Y E S	New thing used in new way	Same thing used in new way
Change in application			
	N O	New thing used in same way	Same thing used in same way (no innovation)

Figure 5-4: Innovation positions.

Building a Better Candle

Many of the participants in our seminars are interested in the Malcolm Baldrige National Quality Award. The Baldrige criteria offer an excellent outline for issues all organizations must address to demonstrate leadership. Our seminar participants often indicate interest in how to guide their organizations to be world-class leaders. To assist their thinking, I give them a simple scenario:

> You are in the top management of a leading candle manufacturer late in the nineteenth century. Your objective is to become the premier best-in-class candle maker. You will achieve this by satisfying customer needs. What attributes of your candles will you improve upon to attain your objective?

Responses to this question immediately erupt. Attributes identified for improvement include:

- Long lasting
- Dripless
- Resistant to deformity
- Scented, smells good
- Many colors
- Brightness
- Smokeless
- Easy lighting

All of these attributes are generated by our natural tendency toward convergent thinking. I tell the participants that, by following this objective, they became a world-class candle maker. But there's a problem. What outcome do customers expect to achieve in using the candle? The unanimous answer is "light."

There are many ways we could pursue this outcome for our customers by thinking divergently: gas lanterns, oil lamps, light bulbs. Unfortunately, the best-in-class candle maker never became a producer of light bulbs. Which market would you prefer to have? We can achieve our objective of being a world-class organization in the short term by thinking convergently. To keep this position on a long-term basis, we are required to think divergently about ways to achieve outcomes customers want. This produces innovation. We can be best in class or create a new class others will covet.

Procter & Gamble is one company that actually had the opportunity to go from candles to light bulbs. It declined Thomas Edison's proposal because the process would require new materials and technology. History was repeated in 1992 with the development of a new type of filament-less bulb that lasts 20 years. It was not developed by General Electric, Phillips, or Sylvania, the current big names in bulbs.

The Frozen Dessert Market

Every industry has a few dominant players. This is certainly true in the fast-food business. When you think of hamburgers, two firms come to mind: McDonald's and Burger King. In chicken, it's Kentucky Fried Chicken. Who would you think of as the major player of the early 1980s in soft-serve frozen dairy desserts? There is a good chance you'd think Dairy Queen, which had the lion's share of the market.

The story today, only a few years later, is quite different. Names like TCBY, Colombo, and McDonald's come to mind. Two of the attributes that make soft-serve dessert "easy to use" are low fat and low calorie. Frozen yogurt is to Dairy Queen as light bulbs are to the candle industry.

The Obsolete Slide Rules

The slide rule was the standard tool for college students in the sciences until the late 1970s. Big names in slide rules included Post, Pickett, and K & E. A quality slide rule was quiet, lightweight, nonwarping, small, and precisely calibrated. Convergent thinking contributed to improvements.

The outcome expected by end-users was to obtain fast, accurate mathematical answers. That outcome is achieved today by electronic calculators at a fraction of the speed, weight, error rate, and cost of slide rules. Innovation by companies like Hewlett-Packard and Texas Instruments made the slide rule and the abacus irrelevant. Abacus makers did not become slide rule producers, and slide rule makers did not eventually make calculators. This historical pattern doesn't project a rosy future for calculator makers unless we change our thinking.

A note regarding technology is in order here. Some readers may be thinking it's unfair to compare slide rules to calculators because each is dependent on distinct technologies. But this is precisely one of the lessons to be learned. Producers care passionately about technologies. Customers care about outcomes. Customers care about technology to the extent that technology improves desired outcomes. The innovative organization that is focused on customers will create, discover, and apply new technologies to achieve new outcomes.

A Revolution in Pharmaceuticals

In the pharmaceutical industry, convergent thinking has been the predominant creator of change in this century until the late 1970s and early 1980s with the rise of companies like Genetech and Biogen. Their innovation in the development of biotechnology is revolutionizing the pharmaceutical industry. Unlike the trial-and-error approach historically used to create new medicines, recombinant genetic engineering is creating cures (and new life forms) by design.

New Thinking for Training Manuals

An illustration of the difference between convergent and divergent thinking occurred when we were working with the training staff of an already quality-conscious equipment manufacturer. The staff had identified one of its training manuals as a service product that needed improvement. Users of the manual could not read well enough to understand how to operate the equipment the manual was addressing. The training staff had decided to rewrite the manual at a lower reading level. We asked them what outcomes they were trying to create with the manual. They wanted manual users to be able to operate the equipment successfully and without damage within x hours. We then asked if they had considered using audiotapes (the equipment operators used Walkman-like radios) or interactive videos plugged into the equipment. They had not. This opened up a whole new avenue to achieve quality training materials. It was also an excellent way to differentiate their equipment from that of the competition.

A Key for Success

At one time American automakers produced over 75 percent of the world's cars. Today, their market share is closer to 30 percent.

There are many reasons for this decline. Not the least of these involves quality. American automakers have been working hard on this issue, with gratifying results. New car warranties reflect the improvement. Prior to 1960, warranties were good for 90 days or 4,000 miles! A typical warranty today for an American-made car is for 50,000 miles and at least three years. Yet J.D. Power Associates reported that new car buyers in 1989 still experienced 163 problems per 100 American cars versus 119 problems per 100 Japanese cars.[1] The United States is getting better, but so are the competitors. Until the latter half of the 1980s, these changes in quality have primarily resulted from convergent thinking.

Quality defined by defects per unit will never enable a producer (except in absence of competition) to achieve or sustain a leadership position. Making defect-free cars is admirable but insufficient. Leadership also requires divergent thinking, with a focus on customers' outcome expectations. The car key is a symbol of how far our thinking has come, as well as how far we need to go.

Users expect that a car key will (1) provide security, and (2) enable vehicle operation. Typical U.S.-made cars require the user to carry two keys—one for the ignition, the other for the door and trunk. Depending on the manufacturer, the keys are either single-sided or double-sided. The user of two single-sided car keys could make four attempts to open the locked car door:

Attempt	Result
1. ignition key in "down" position	no entry
2. ignition key in "up" position	no entry
3. door key in "down" position	no entry
4. door key in "up" position	entry

The user of two double-sided keys may potentially make two attempts to open the locked car door:

Attempt	Result
1. ignition key	no entry
2. door key	entry

Virtually all car manufacturers outside the United States provide users with *one* key that operates everything. No matter which way you insert the key, you are always right. The Japanese call this concept poka-yoke (mistake-proof). The Germans and Japanese have been building one-key cars for over 20 years! Why is it that American producers still haven't gotten the picture?

The convergent approach to improvement is illustrated by shaping the two keys differently. The divergent approach to improvement focuses on customers' desired outcomes and develops products to better achieve them. One double-sided key also addresses three of the important attributes all customers want in all products: ease of use, timeliness, and certainty. In this example, we could even throw in a producer-desired attribute, cost, and see that one key performs better than two.

General Motors gave its employees a Christmas present in December 1991: It announced that more than 74,000 employees would lose their jobs in the next few years. What is the role of single-sided keys? During the same time frame (1991 to 1992), GM's Opel cars were hot in Europe; their new Saturn cars are in high demand in the United States. *Both use a single double-sided key.* Customers don't buy cars just because of the key; it is only one of many symptoms of the way we think about customer needs, and only one reason why U.S. customers buy imports.

Traditional quality management is product-focused. The new quality management must be outcome-focused as well. How can we combine the two?

We must first determine what results customers want to achieve by using our current (or prospective) product. We start by defining expected outcomes. Suppose we produce a financial report for others within our organization. We would identify who the report's end-users are and ask "Why do you use this product?" and "How do you use this product?"

OUTCOME-FOCUSED DIVERGENT THINKING

It's always easier to laugh at the dumb things others do; our challenge is to avoid the mistakes of the slide rule makers and their kind by rethinking why we do what we do. Exercise 6 should help.

Many people find this exercise difficult because it requires divergent thinking. Remember, innovation can occur by happy coincidence or by design; this exercise helps you begin the innovation process by design. Before you begin, consider the differences between outcomes desired by customers and those desired by producers.

An outcome desired by a customer is:	An outcome desired by a producer is:
• Independent of a specific product	• Dependent on a specific product
• A condition that is personally experienced	• A condition which is organizationally and/or personally experienced
• Stable over time, though the definition may change	• Changeable over time
• The primary reason for using a product	• The primary reason for producing a product

Table 5-1: Comparing desired outcomes.

You identified a target product in Chapter 1. You can continue to use it for this exercise. Involve a small group of interested others, especially end-users, if possible. You may be surprised to discover that those with the least detailed knowledge of the product can most quickly identify customer outcomes. The key to success is to focus on the *results* intended by use of this product, not the product's characteristics or features. The example given earlier of the training manual product shows outcome-focused divergent thinking. Table 5-2 gives additional illustrations.

EXERCISE 6: OUTCOMES

	Expected time (minutes)
Instructions:	
1. Each person on the team is responsible for recording notes. Assign a timekeeper.	
2. Write in the name of the target product, producer, and end-user customer	2
3. Divide the team in half. Half the team addresses customer's desired and undesired outcomes (boxes 1 and 2); the other half of team does the same for the producer (boxes 3 and 4).	
Outcomes refers to *results* obtained by using the product, not characteristics of the product. In other words, outcomes are not product-specific. (For instance, "health" is an outcome. Many products contribute to the achievement of health.) If any statement written in one of the four outcome boxes applies only to the target product, it is not an outcome.	
Use the following example attributes:	
a. A quality ___(product)___ results in ___(desired outcome)___ (boxes 1 and 3).	
b. A quality ___(product)___ does not result in _(undesired outcome)_ (boxes 2 and 4).	
Outcome attributes, desired or undesired, cannot begin with negative prefixes or words such as: • un (unpaid) • no (no loss) • in (inaccurate) • dis (dissatisfaction) • non (nonconformance)	30
4. Combine both halves of the team. Rank the customer's desired and undesired outcomes in order of customer priority; 1 = most important. Repeat the process to rank producer priorities.	6
5. Which of the four outcome boxes does your current organizational mission primarily address?	
	2
6. Summarize your experience by answering these questions: a. How many total outcomes were identified for the customer; for the producer? b. What were the two most important customer outcomes? c. What were the two most important producer outcomes? d. Which of the outcomes named in 6b and 6c are presently measured? How? e. What discoveries did you make? f. What actions should/will you take?	20
Total estimated minutes	60

7. What alternatives to the current product could better achieve the customer's desired outcomes?

Target product

	Desired outcomes (outcomes wanted)	Undesired outcomes (outcomes not wanted)
Customer	①	②
Producer	③	④

Sample products	Possible outcomes			
	Wanted by customer	Not wanted by customer	Wanted by producer	Not wanted by producer
Slide rule	Fast, accurate calculations	Bulky objects; limited application	Steady profits; predictable production	Loss of market share
8mm movie film	Clear, accurate, complete recording of important events; permanent reference	Out-of-focus images; lost film; faded images	Steady profits; predictable production; virtual monopoly of market	Changes in film formats; ecological complaints; "expired film"
Tallow candles	Light	Fires; sooty air; stained furniture	Steady profits; predictable production	Premature melting; lawsuits; electrification
Belted ply auto tires with inner tubes	Versatile, safe transportation; low operating cost	Blowouts; poor handling; limited operating condition	Steady profits; minimum number of standardized sizes; heavy cars	Product recalls; controlled supplies; changes in manufacturing tooling requirements
Hard rubber auto battery cases	Dependable car starting; low operating cost	Acid leaks; extra weight	Cold weather; steady profits; largest containers	Lawsuits; returned batteries; changes in car design requirements
Iceboxes	Preserved food; convenience	Frequent shopping; messes; bad smells	Steady profits; hot weather	Consumes electricity; loss of ice supplies

Table 5-2: Illustration of outcome-focused divergent thinking.

Conclusion

Your experience with Exercise 6 may be similar to that of our clients. Discoveries stated by our workshop participants include the following:

- We had a hard time focusing on product outcomes. Our tendency was to write down product attributes instead.
- Our current organizational mission emphasizes producer interests (boxes 3 and 4).
- Most of our quality improvement effects are aimed at fixing underserved producer outcomes (box 4).

- We don't measure our fulfillment of customers' desired outcomes.
- There is a mismatch between our formally stated mission and actual behavior.
- Incentives are related to everything *except* customers' desired outcomes.
- Our mission is producer-centered.
- It is easier to identify producer outcomes than those customers want.
- Our organization is spending very little effort to identify or develop other products that could better achieve the outcomes both our customers want and we want.

Quality is product-focused and is influenced by industry (producer) standards and current technology. Improvements tend to be made incrementally, using convergent thinking. The traditional questions being asked are "Does this product meet measurable specifications?" and "How can we apply continuous improvement?"

Benchmarking can help break the convergent thinking paradigm. Modeling a function's operations after others that are perceived as "best in class" can result in a fast change to a new standard. That's the good news. Unfortunately, convergent thinking can easily take root again. Done well, benchmarking must include in-depth discussion with customers to understand the outcomes they want to achieve and those they want to avoid.

Benchmarking, once completed, guarantees neither continual improvement nor innovation. At best, it can uncover how to be equal to the best. Continuous innovation, actively involving customers and focused on their expectations, can achieve and sustain leadership. Guidelines on how to sell your innovations are outlined below.

Ten Tactics for Reducing Resistance to Innovation*

1. *Perceived advantage:* The user should easily see an advantage of the innovation over the current practice.

2. *Compatibility:* The better the new idea is perceived to fit with what is already being done, the more likely it is that it will be accepted.

---

*Originally based on research on the diffusion of innovations by Dr. Everett Rogers: an abstract from a forthcoming book by James R. Bright on Strategy and Tactics in Innovation. Published by the Institute of Electrical and Electronic Engineers (IEE)—From Proceeding of PICMAT '91, Portland, OR "Strategies to Speed the Adoption of Innovation," paper IDA608 Portland, OR.

3. *Simplicity:* Keep the supporting activity as simple as possible. This doesn't mean the mechanism should not be complex. It merely means the user's perception of the innovation should be simple.

4. *Divisibility:* The more the innovation can be tried one piece at a time, the easier it will be accepted.

5. *Communicability:* If you use old vocabulary to describe the new idea, you make it easier to accept.

6. *Reversibility:* It must be easy for the user to withdraw from the use of the innovation.

7. *Relative costliness:* The degree to which the innovation absorbs the user's resources—including time, money, personpower, emotional commitment, and so on—should be less than what it is replacing.

8. *Credibility:* How does the user feel about the innovator? Are you trustworthy? Do you have a reputation that supports the innovation? The better your reputation is in the field of the innovation, the better off you are.

9. *Reliability:* Will it work right the first time? This requirement is quite new. Until recently, it was assumed that the first one would have some troubles. But, now, because of Japanese competition and generally higher quality standards, the user expects that it wouldn't be brought to the market unless it worked the way it is supposed to. No prototypes, please.

10. *Failure consequences:* The user must understand the consequences of failure of the innovation and, obviously, the less potential injury from failure, the more interested the user will be.

Remember, the key is how the user perceives the impact of the innovation, not how you, the innovator, perceive it.

Notes

1. Thomas McCarroll, "The Supply-Side Scourge," *Time*, 13 November, 1989, 81.

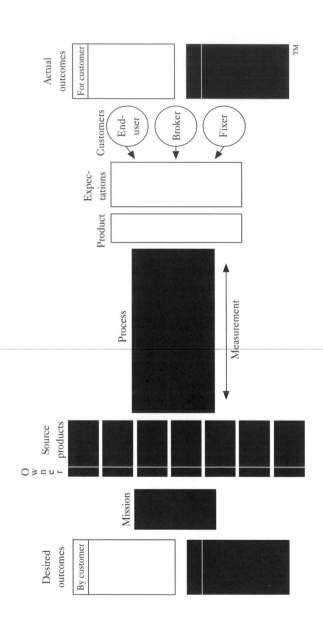

The Customer-Centered Culture Model™

6

Process

Everything we've discussed so far addressed "doing the right thing." The "right thing" requires understanding what others want from the things we create for them. The focus has been on the design of service products. If the product isn't designed well to start with, then concern with how we produce it is irrelevant.

The old masters—especially Deming, Crosby, Ishikawa, Armand Feigenbaum, and Joseph Juran—have primarily emphasized process. I believe there are two major reasons for this. First, the old masters received their formative professional development as members of manufacturing organizations. Management concerns in the industrial age, initially embodied in the ideas of Frederick Taylor, had a lot to do with methods of production. Even today, the quality literature is heavily focused on manufacturing and production technologies. We can't say product design was disregarded, but it appears to have received less attention. The old masters are products of their time. It seems they assumed products were well designed, just poorly produced. The huge demand for all types of American products after World War II reinforced that assumption: Everything made was sold. The abundance of natural resources available to U.S. manufacturers helped to make volume, and to a lesser extent cost, the major forces in business performance in the 25 years after the war.

In Japan, the lack of natural resources and the need to rebuild manufacturing capacity required great attention to productivity. Certainly in those early years, we could argue that design was not perceived as one of Japan's strong suits. Until the mid-1960s, much of Japan's success rested on its ability to take others' designs and excel at producing them efficiently. Product design technology began to emerge in Japan in 1972 with the arrival of Yoji Akao on the scene at Kobe shipyards. Akao's methods have been labeled QFD. Chapters 3 and 4 incorporate some of his concepts and apply them to service. This is the new wave regarding quality management.

The second reason why the old masters focused so heavily on process was the traditional role of the quality assurance function in manufacturing. This group was primarily involved in inspecting finished goods. Products that didn't meet certain standards were sent back for rework; the rest were sent on to customers. The old masters appropriately argued that the production process should be run so that defective products were caught much further upstream. Their focus was aimed at reducing the cost of poor quality, based on technical product criteria. There is proportionately little mention by the old masters in pre-1980 writings regarding quality from the customer's perspective. Juran addresses this somewhat more than the others.

As the United States began to awaken in the 1980s to the realities of limited resources, a global market, and strong international competition, the need to readdress quality grew stronger. Unfortunately, we have continued to focus almost exclusively on process issues with the same traditional tools used for the past 40 years. After the 1980 broadcast of the NBC White Paper program "If Japan Can, Why Can't We?," the United States began importing these techniques and tools. Remember quality circles? They worked so well in Japan that they were quickly identified as "the answer." Juran had been instrumental in helping the Japanese establish these teams to teach problem-solving techniques. Our experience in the United States was that, while these teams could help with problems at a work group level, they were not the solution we thought they would be.

The first few years of the 1980s saw the emergence of Crosby (*Quality Is Free*, 1979) and Deming (*Quality, Productivity and Competitive Position*, 1982). Crosby's masterful contribution was to focus executives' attention on the dollar impact of poor quality. Crosby's 14 steps laid out topics to be addressed for quality awareness. Deming, like Juran, had established his credibility through work with the Japanese. His contribution was in popularizing the power of statistical methods for the control of process variability. Deming's 14 points summarized his philosophy regarding management practices.

The teachings of these masters, each in their turn, have been adopted as additional "answers" to dilemmas of quality and competitiveness. In 1985, Ishikawa published his English translation of *What Is Total Quality Control? The Japanese Way*. Finally, we had a Japanese master revealing the secrets of how to do things. Ishikawa helped us see that we had been acting as the proverbial blind men in describing the elephant by the part being held at the moment. Ishikawa said that quality, like the elephant, must be understood by seeing all of its parts. Unfortunately, "control" is one of those words that fails to capture the imagination. With a little modification, we were able to repackage total quality control as total quality management and get to where we are today. To summarize this journey, we might say that quality has become more fully understood through a series of progressive revelations. These revelations have become popularly acknowledged as "the way" at least 20 years after their initial inception. Deming began preaching his path for enlightenment in the late 1940s. Ishikawa was making his way as a consultant to major Japanese firms in the 1950s and early 1960s. Akao began teaching his methods in the early 1970s.

Our challenge today is to integrate what we've learned (or should have learned) from the past while leapfrogging the normal 20-year delay from revelation to application. To do this, in process applications, we must completely rethink our understanding of what process means. Just as we started out in Chapter 1 by rethinking what service means, we have to set aside old notions. We redefined service as products. We need to redefine process.

Although each of the old masters has his own view of process (see Figure 6-1), I have found it helpful to define process two ways, as given in Figure 6-2.

REDEFINING PROCESS

It is unfortunate that many people have equated total quality management with the tools of statistical process control. The logical extension of this thinking has overemphasized the use of control charting techniques. This has resulted in drawing the absurd conclusion that our primary objective is to limit variation within a process. In its most simplistic terms, this can be (and is) misunderstood to mean that if the industry standard is to

- Deming: "Every activity, every job is part of a process." (*Out of the Crisis*, 1982)

- Crosby: "A process is a series of actions or operations conducted to produce a desired result." (*Quality Improvement Through Defect Prevention*, 1985)

- Juran: "A process is a systematic series of actions directed to the achievement of a goal." (*Juran on Planning for Quality*, 1988)

- Fukuda: "Process refers to the flow of materials." (*Management Engineering*, 1983) Ryuji Fukuda is the developer of the CEDAC (Cause and Effect Diagrams with the Addition of Cards) method of problem solving.

- Ishikawa: "Process is a collection of cause factors." (*What Is Total Quality Control? The Japanese Way*, 1984)

Figure 6-1: Process as defined by the old masters.

1. For the entire enterprise, its major organizational units, and individuals, *a process is the flow of products* organized to achieve customer satisfaction with the final product.

2. For individuals and natural work groups, *a process is also the sequence of activities* that creates a product.

Figure 6-2: Lawton's process definitions.

have airplanes arrive within 15 minutes of the scheduled time, we are "in control" and doing well if 99.9 percent of the airline's flights meet that objective. Several potential problems with this thinking are revealed by the following questions.

- To what degree does the industry standard for "on-time" performance reflect customer expectations?
- In this case, are consistency and predictability equivalent to quality?
- How does this performance contribute to an individual airline's competitiveness?

- To what extent does on-time arrival contribute to the customer's total satisfaction? Does it account for 2 percent or 50 percent of satisfaction?

My point is that to address quality, we should not begin with stability in the process; we should start with *time*. The objective is to cut as much time from the process as possible. Since we're talking about the need to change our thinking about process, we may as well go all the way and address how much time to cut.

TIME-BASED PROCESS IMPROVEMENT

If your organization is engaged in some form of continuous improvement, how much time do you think is reasonable to remove from a process on your first improvement effort? Consider the corporate requisition process for buying a personal computer. How long does it take from the time you generate the request until the computer arrives on your desk? Now consider your objective of removing time consumption from this process.

Using a continuous improvement philosophy, how much time could you cut on your first try? How will statistical process control techniques help?

Most people respond by saying 10 to 35 percent of the time could be cut out. *Continuous improvement* is another one of those phrases which may inadvertently guide us to the wrong objectives. Make it your objective to *cut 80 percent of the total time* (as perceived by the customer) on your first attempt at process improvement. It should be absolutely clear that convergent thinking, implied by the phrase *continuous improvement*, is not going to enable a change of this magnitude on your first try. Statistical methods are of little help. The whole process has to be completely rethought, using divergent thinking. In *Competing Against Time*, George Stalk and Thomas Hout provide a wealth of evidence to confirm my experience that only .05 to 5 percent of a normal business process consists of value-added time. In other words, 95 to 99.95 percent of the total time is wasted.

An example of this enormous potential exists in the airline industry. Statistical measures have been in place for years regarding the variation in "service time" a customer experiences at the check-in counter. A typical standard is that the reservation agent should be able, on average, to handle each customer's needs within three minutes. Their statistics may show that this process is stable or "in control." The problem is that customers may spend 30 minutes or more in line waiting to get to the check-in counter. The customer's experience of the "check-in" time begins when he/she arrives at the terminal and ends when he/she leaves the check-in counter with a seat assignment and claim tags for checked luggage. The three minutes spent at the counter are irrelevant compared with the total time of thirty minutes or more. In this case, three minutes is 10 percent of the total time which adds value. Could 80 percent of the total time be cut? Using divergent thinking, how many ways can we devise to do this?

Part of our management challenge is to include the customer's perception of time in the objectives established for processes. Almost invariably, time standards focus on the producer's part of the process. This is not true only of airlines. One of our clients is a major retailer whose management had developed a standard called "one plus one." This refers to the checkout line in the store. As one customer is checking out, no more than one customer should be waiting in line. This standard was a reflection of the progressive attitude of management toward its customers. However, to include the total customer experience with process time, we'd have to start the clock when the customer arrives at the parking lot and stop the clock when the customer returns to the car with his/her purchases. When this is done, we find a host of previously ignored opportunities. They are uncovered by answering questions like these.

- How can the store layout and aisle labeling be changed to shorten shopping time? (How does this compete with the retailer's desires?)
- What is the current ratio of number of items purchased to total process time? What could it be? (For example, if it takes 75 minutes to buy six items, what consumes most of this time and what changes can reduce it?)

Not only can we cut the time from most processes by 80 percent on our first try, the attitude necessary to pursue this goal will also lead to other breakthroughs. Another example can illustrate this.

The Long-Delayed Retirement Checks
The new CEO of a 45,000-person corporation received complaints from recent retirees who were unhappy that it took over two months to obtain their first retirement checks. After employees had worked for the

company for 25 years, this pause of income was not exactly the "thank you" they wanted. The executive vice president for human resources was asked to find out how things could be improved.

A cross-functional team of seven people was established, representing the benefits, employee records, information systems, and related departments. The team used the methods outlined in this book to (1) find out what customers (retirees) wanted regarding the retirement process, and (2) figure out how to shorten the process. We gave them the objective of 80 percent time reduction, just to get one aspect of the vision clearly stated. (It also gets the adrenaline flowing appropriately.)

The team used the FACT sheet tool, shown in Figure 6-3, to identify the flow of the current process quickly. The FACT sheet is a mapping tool that identifies which *functions* are involved in the process, what *activities* they perform, and how much *time* is consumed. The team's immediate discoveries included the following.

- The total process cycle took 124 to 253 days and consisted of over 200 steps.
- Five hours and 16 minutes of value-adding time (when actual work was done) were consumed in getting out the first retirement check (no more than 0.5 percent of the total cycle time).
- The timing of batches within the process prevented reduction of more than 10 percent of the total time unless the process was redesigned.
- A great deal of redundancy was occurring: the principles of "just-in-case" outweighed thinking based on just-in-time principles.

One of the most striking revelations concerned the very first product created at the beginning of the process. This was a report produced at the beginning of each year that contained the names and birth dates of all employees reaching normal retirement age (at 65) during the year. This report was the basis for sending out preretirement information to prospective retirees. One of the team's key discoveries was that since over 80 percent of employees took early retirement (beginning at age 55), this first report was created up to 10 years late! Consequently, the processing of most retirements occurred reactively. Some of the team's other discoveries and the whole project process are expanded upon in Chapter 7. The team's FACT sheets in Figure 6-4 show one of the important process tools used.

FACT SHEET Function, activity and time   Page 1 of 2

① Final product: *Retiree check*
② Initial product: *Retiree list*
③ Process ends when: *Retiree receives first check*
④ Process begins when: *Retire to get forms is listed*
⑤ How long does it presently take to go from 4 to 3? a. Best case ____ b. Worst case ____ c. Average ____

⑥ Function	⑦ Activity	⑧ Min. VAT	⑩ Cycle	Best/worst ⑩ days
6a *Customer* Retiree	3)30 30-90 Retiree completes forms	30	30	90
6b Employee records	1)10 3-4 Lists retirees to get forms; 6)60 3-15 Processes retirement forms; 7)0 1-2 Delivers forms to pensions	70	7	21
6c Benefits	2)10 3 Sends letter/ forms to retiree	10	3	3
6d Retirement communi-cations	4)10 1-10 Reviews completed forms	10	1	10
6e Retiree's manager	5)10 45-60 Prepares PAN	10	45	60
	⑨			⑪

■ Current   □ Proposed

Figure 6-3: FACT sheet.

FACT SHEET Function, activity and time   Page 2 of 2

(1) Final product: *Retiree check*
(2) Initial product: *Retiree list*
(3) Process ends when: *Retiree receives first check*
(4) Process begins when: *Retire to get forms is listed*
(5) How long does it presently take to go from 4 to 3? a. Best case ____ b. Worst case ____ c. Average ____

(6) Function	(7) Activity					(8) Min. VAT	(10) Cycle	Best/ worst (10) days
6a *Customer* Retiree								
						5	3	5
6b Insurance	8)15 2 Adds auto insurance					15	2	2
6c Pensions	9)5 1-2 Files form logs and	10c)5 1/2-1 Requests pension statement	11)50 Does calculation	12a)30 1-10 Prepares input form thru Fed Ex	13)6 4-8 Prepares reconciliation report	96	6.5	21
6d Information systems		10b)15 4-8 Updates pension system w/payroll data				15	4	8
6e Payroll		10a)45 13-21 Processes payroll data				45	13	21
6f Trustee				12b)7 4 Inputs data	14)3 8 Produces retirement check	10	10	12

Explanation

13 refers to the activity number
4-8 refers to the time work is occurring
(VAT) in minutes refers to the total cycle time of the activity, including delays, transportation, etc. in days refers to the activity

■ Current □ Proposed   VAT = .5% of Cycle   Total VAT (9) 5 hrs 16 min   124.5 / 253 (11)

Figure 6-3 (Continued): FACT sheet.

FACT SHEET Function, activity and time

① Final product: *Retiree check*
② Initial product: *Retirement ltr/forms/report/stmt*
⑤ How long does it presently take to go from 4 to 3? a. Best case ____ b. Worst case ____ c. Average ____

③ Process ends when: *Retiree receives first check*
④ Process begins when: *RC sends ltr/forms to retiree*

Page 1 of 2

⑥ Function	⑦ Activity			⑧ Min. VAT	⑩ Cycle Best/worst days
6a *Customer* Retiree	3)15 1-14 Completes forms			15	1 / 14
6b Retirement communications	2)4 1-1 Sends ltr/forms to retiree			4	1 / 1
6c Insurance		5)10 1/2-1 Determines ins rates/notifies pensions		10	.5 / 1
6d Pensions		4)5 1/2-3 Reviews completed forms	6)20 1/2-10 Prepares input 7)10 1/2-7 Prepares PAN	35	1.5 / 20
6e Information systems	1)5 1/2-1 Generates report\ltr forms/stmt			5	.5 / 1
6f Payroll				0	0
6g Trustee				0	0
	⑨				⑪

□ Current ■ Proposed   Prepared by _____

Figure 6-4

FACT SHEET Function, activity and time Page 2 of 2

① Final product: *Retiree check*
② Initial product: *Retirement Inf/forms/report/stmt*
③ Process ends when: *Retiree receives first check*
④ Process begins when: *RC sends Inf/forms to retiree*
⑤ How long does it presently take to go from 4 to 3? a. Best case ___ b. Worst case ___ c. Average ___

⑥ Function	⑦ Activity			⑧ Min. VAT	⑩ Cycle (Best/worst days)
6a *Customer* Retiree			11b)3 | 8 Receives check	5	3 / 5
6b Retirement communications				0	0
6c Insurance				0	0
6d Pensions	8c)5 | 1/2-1 Receives pension requested stmt	9)30 | 1-3 Does calculation	10)3 | 2-6 Prepares reconciliation report	38	3.5 / 10
6e Information systems	8b)5 | 1-3 Updates pension system w/pay data			5	1 / 3
6f Payroll	8a)5 | 1-15 Processes payroll data	11a)7 | 4 Inputs data	11b)3 | 8 Produces retiree check	45	1 / 15
6g Trustee				10	12 / 12
				2 hrs. 52 min	24.5 / 82

Total VAT ⑨ ___ ⑪

☐ Current ■ Proposed   Prepared by ___

Figure 6-4 (Continued)

The team ultimately redesigned the process so the first retirement check was routinely deposited in the retiree's bank on the day after retirement. This redesign enabled as much as 99 percent of the customer-experienced cycle time to be cut. The methods the pension check team used have created similar impressive results for all sorts of team projects we've worked with. The steps are outlined in Table 6-1.

---

1. Map the process.

2. Measure time, cost, and yield.

3. Modify batch size and timing.

4. Remove inspectors.

5. Process in parallel.

6. Increase precision and certainty.

Table 6-1: Time-based process improvement.

The "Secret" PC Approval Process

Another story will provide the context for discussing these process improvement strategies. A number of years ago, I worked with a division of a 60,000-person technology company. The division's problem was that its personnel couldn't get PC requisitions approved in a timely way, and many were not approved at all. As initially stated by management, the problem had two parts: timeliness and yield (the percent that were approved). The division's top management asked for help. It viewed the PCs as essential tools in maintaining competiveness in its business. My job was to figure out why the problem existed and propose action to remedy it. The target product was the PC requisition. The target process was the requisition approval process.

Like most processes in complex organizations, this one cut across vertical structures (often called silos) of the organization. My first step was to figure out the path of the requisition from initiation to approval. It became clear immediately that no one owned (or would claim responsibility for) the whole process. It also became obvious that each requisition was handcrafted its own unique way.

Each requisition went through a series of approval steps. In many cases, the requisition was reviewed by several department heads, at least once by one of the division's executives, and by two or more people at the corporate level; finally, it might arrive on the desk of an executive corporate vice president. This requisition process was not a straight line between two points. A majority of the requisitions were returned to the originator for revisions at least once. The reasons for the revisions included second-guessing by the various approvers of what subsequent approvers might want to see in the requisition. Each of these approvals was really an inspection point; the approvers were acting as "inspectors." Several of these requisition inspectors explained to me that they were unsure of the basis for final approval. There were no written approval criteria.

Finally, the executive vice president and I were able to meet. I asked if he could tell me what he required of a requisition before he approved it. His reply was, "I'm sorry, but that's confidential." I wasn't sure I'd heard him right. As politely as possible, I asked, "Excuse me, did you say that your requirements for approval are a secret?"

"We have very limited resources available for PCs," he said, "yet we are getting hundreds of requests for PCs from all over the corporation. If we told everyone what the criteria for approval, they'd all write their requisitions to meet the criteria. We'd go broke buying PCs."

I asked, "Couldn't you communicate your approval criteria and indicate that approvals would be granted on a first-come, first-served basis until the limited funds were gone?"

"No, no," he replied. "We're comfortable with things as they are. You have to understand that my job is to protect corporate assets."

I guess he told me! I couldn't very well go back to the division management empty-handed so I knew there had to be another way. As all of us who've ever sought change in organizations know, ideas for improvements have a better chance of management acceptance if they address the two things management cares about most: time and money. So I went back to the drawing board, literally. I mapped the whole PC requisition process to identify who did what. I then determined the cost of the process by quantifying who spent how much time and at what rate of pay. The "inspectors" were all managers. The key discovery: The average labor cost to create and process a PC requisition (with or without final approval) was *five times* the cost of the average PC.

We might ask whose "assets" the executive vice president really was protecting. Certainly not the corporation's. This is another instance of using a vital lie ("to protect corporate assets") to maintain the status quo or one's posterior. The epilogue is that things finally did change. The pace of change quickened once the executive vice president was moved to another position. As you might imagine, this problem was not the only factor in his ultimate departure, nor was that ever an objective of the project. The objective was to improve the timeliness, cost, and yield of the process to address customer and business needs better.

How is this story relevant to your own experiences and observations in your organization? Let's explore the six steps in achieving time-based process improvement.

MAPPING THE PROCESS

Mapping or flowcharting a process is essential for truly understanding the current state of affairs. Just mapping the "as is" process reveals how much we don't know. When a cross-functional team does this, team members ask each other many penetrating questions which begin with "Why?" Answers like "Because we've always done it that way" are not acceptable.

A process can be mapped to show the flow of products, activities, information, and decisions. For our purposes, we'll focus on the flow of products and activities. The following are some of the main purposes of mapping.

- Document the "as is" (current) process for analysis.
- Identify process ownership and roles.
- Define the relationship among products and activities.
- Identify bottlenecks, the critical path, and disconnects (places where things fall through cracks in the process).
- Determine the difference between cycle time and value-added time.
- Establish a basis for measuring process performance.
- Take action, then evaluate the results.
- Measure process performance.
- Prioritize improvement opportunities.
- Take action.

The processes with greatest potential for improvement, for both the customer's and producer's benefit, are those that cut across functional groups. The customer order process would be an example. Typical functions involved include sales, data processing, scheduling, engineering, distribution/shipping, and customer service. One of the major challenges is to identify who owns these cross-functional processes. Ownership means that one person has the clearly recognized responsibility for all the resources required by the process and is accountable for its performance.

In a very small organization, the president may be the owner of many of the major business processes. Complex organizations frequently have fragmented process ownership. This is especially evident when something goes wrong and it isn't clear who is the responsible party.

Process ownership should go hand in hand with product ownership. Some organizations have used the product line manager role to establish ownership of both product and process. However, the product line manager who has responsibility without resources and authority doesn't really have ownership. Such positions can make a person feel like a eunuch. 3M is a good example of an organization structured by product and process, yet even there, breakdowns tend to occur on cross-group processes.

Exercises at the end of this chapter use two important tools: the FACT sheet and the product-roles matrix.

The product-roles matrix uncovers the flow of products within the process and their relationship with participants in the process. Identifying the product flow can help prioritize improvement opportunities. For example, in the pension check project cited earlier, the first product in the process was a report whose content and timing had a major negative effect on the pension check (the final product in the process). This report had to be completely redesigned to streamline the pension check process significantly. In both service and manufacturing organizations, the flow of products has everything to do with time-based process improvement.

Our three improvement principles regarding both process activities and product flow within a process are the following:

1. Eliminate
2. Consolidate
3. Automate (only if it adds value)

It is critical to pursue these principles in the order stated. Many organizations have a history of applying them in reverse order. In our eagerness to apply technology to business needs, we frequently automate the current process with many of its inherent problems unchanged. Changing the process after it has been automated is financially and politically difficult.

A classic example of elimination and consolidation was Motorola's electronic pagers. Only a few years ago, it took about three weeks from the time a customer placed an order to the time the pager was shipped. Today, pagers can be shipped within about an hour. This radical change in responsiveness was not created by adding to inventory. It involved redesigning the pager to contain fewer parts and redesigning the assembly and order process to eliminate steps. Mapping was instrumental in achieving these results.

It is not sufficient to improve an activity. Our first step is to challenge our reason for doing it at all.

Conversely, it is common to find that we are not doing something that is needed. Every process needs a guiding document that clearly addresses the process' intent and desired outcome. Such guiding documents can be policies, strategies, or plans. I call them *source products*. These are the source from which all processes flow. Source products provide the bridge between an organization's mission and its operations. They are usually the responsibility of upper management, the process owners.

One important source product in most companies is the sales forecast. The forecast is usually created by the marketing or sales organization monthly or quarterly, and an annual forecast helps other internal functions develop budgets, schedules, staffing plans, and so on. Most people agree that a sales forecast is likely to be fairly accurate for no more than three months following its development. From there on, it gets increasingly inaccurate.

If this is true, why do we create the forecast annually and pretend it represents truth? We could admit that it has a short shelf life and only produce one monthly or quarterly. Senior management is responsible for assuring this product has meaning for its end-users. If the sales forecast is not right, how can anything which flows from it (budgets, schedules) be right?

Another important source product is the organization's quality policy. If the organization doesn't have one, there will be little consensus on what quality means. Even the organization which has a quality policy still has not achieved much if the policy is vague, inconsistently applied, unused, or not tied to relevant performance measures.

Top managers who are concerned with process improvement have the challenge to address the design and quality of their source products. Source products create the foundation for effective processes.

Consider the process your business uses for translating a customer need into an order. Who owns that process? A sales manager is probably the

---

Quality Policy

All International Management Technologies, Inc. partners, employees, and associates will use every means possible to convey personal concerns for our customers' satisfaction. We will demonstrate that commitment by consistently taking the following actions.

- Solicit customer needs and expectations.
- Confirm that we have understood those expectations.
- Develop, package, deliver, and support IMT products to meet those expectations.
- Measure the degree to which our customers' product and outcome expectations are achieved.
- Accept full responsibility for reducing any gap between what our customers expect and what they experience.

Figure 6-5: Source product example.

owner. There may be a procedure outlining the steps to be taken. Is there a source product that outlines the intent of the process and the desired outcomes expected by both the customer and the process contributors? Is your answer representative of most other processes in the organization? Mapping helps identify the extent to which the process's purpose is being achieved.

This is a good time to stop and complete the FACT sheet and process-roles matrix exercises at the end of this chapter for the process that creates the target product you identified in Chapter 1.

MEASURING TIME

There are two types of time consumed by a process: cycle time and value-added time.

Cycle time (CT) refers to the total elapsed time of the process.

Value-added time (VAT) is the amount of labor time consumed in the process, including both the producer's and the customer's labor. Please note that the term, as normally used, does not necessarily represent a judgment that the work being done is actually of value.

Let's take an example. If a life insurance policy is the product, we could call the related process the life insurance policy issuing process. From the producer's perspective, cycle time would begin when the insurance application is received in the home office and end when the approved policy is mailed out. This cycle time might be 15 days. Of course, if we have a customer-centered culture, we have to consider cycle time from the customer's perspective. That would begin when the prospective policy owner expresses interest in having the life insurance policy and end when the customer receives the approved policy. This cycle time might be 60 days.

From the producer's perspective, value-added time would include all the work the insurance company pays its employees to perform, such as:

- Receiving and sorting the application in the mail room
- Screening the application for completeness and accuracy
- Reviewing the applicant's health history
- Underwriting the policy
- Establishing a customer file and payment schedule
- Sending the policy to the customer and copies to various internal departments
- Filing the policy copies

The total VAT, not counting delays or waiting, might be two hours.

The comparable VAT from the customer's perspective would include the following:

- Meeting with the insurance company representative
- Filling out the forms
- Getting a medical examination
- Organizing and sending medical and personal records to the insurance company
- Calling to find out the status of the policy
- Receiving, reviewing, and filing the policy

The total work time the customer spends could be six hours. Do you think the producers know this or have accounted for this customer activity in the design of the process? Probably not.

As producers, we generally measure very little about the customers' total experience with time. We may know about parts of their experience, at best. The Internal Revenue Service is required by law to address tax form simplicity. Even if we don't think the forms are easy to use, at least the IRS provides us with an example of how to address customers' experience of time (see Table 6-2).

The time needed to complete and file the following forms will vary depending on individual circumstances. The estimated average times are given.

Form	Recordkeeping	Learning about the law or the form	Preparing the form	Copying, assembling, and sending the form to the IRS
1040	3 hours, 8 min.	2 hours, 33 min.	3 hours, 17 min.	35 min.
Sch. A (1040)	2 hours, 32 min.	25 min.	56 min.	20 min.
Sch. B (1040)	33 min.	10 min.	17 min.	20 min.
Sch. C (1040)	6 hours, 13 min.	1 hour, 5 min.	1 hour, 56 min.	25 min.
Sch. D (1040)	51 min.	56 min.	56 min.	35 min.
Sch. D-1 (1040)	13 min.	1 min.	13 min.	35 min.
Sch. E (1040)	2 hours, 52 min.	1 hour, 6 min.	1 hour, 16 min.	35 min.
Sch. F (1040) Cash method Accrual method	 4 hours, 2 min. 4 hours, 22 min.	 34 min. 26 min.	 1 hour, 17 min. 1 hour, 19 min.	 20 min. 20 min.
Sch. R (1040)	20 min.	15 min.	21 min.	35 min.
Sch. SE (1040) Short form Long form	 20 min. 26 min.	 12 min. 22 min.	 14 min. 40 min.	 14 min. 20 min.

Source: 1990 IRS 1040 Instructions, Page 4

Table 6-2: IRS estimate of customers' expended time to file taxes.

The customer-centered culture will work to improve and measure cycle time and expended time experienced by both the producer and customer. The FACT sheet is one tool that can help.

Precision and Certainty

Cycle time and VAT tend to address the *duration* of time—that is, how long something takes. In many cases, measuring *precision* regarding time is also important. Suppose you have a problem with your home phone's operation on Saturday morning. You call the phone company (from your neighbor's phone) to arrange to have it fixed. The customer service people tell you they'll send someone out on Tuesday between 9 A.M. and 4 P.M. They say the repair should take no more than an hour. You are required to be at home to let the repairperson in. On Monday, you cancel all your meetings and commitments planned for Tuesday. The repairperson arrives on Tuesday at 11:45 A.M. and is able to fix the problem (a faulty phone line) by 12:20 P.M.

The total cycle time is 42 hours, from the time the problem was discovered to the time it was fixed. You may have two complaints: (1) the length of time to respond to your need (duration), and (2) the estimate of the repairperson's arrival time (precision). Even if the phone company didn't shorten the time to arrive, their ability to tell you the repairperson would be there between 11 A.M. and 1 P.M. could have saved most of your lost work day. The phone company's knowledge about the process and its communication of this would increase your feeling of certainty. This attention to both duration and precision of process time is what helped Domino's Pizza differentiate itself.

MEASURING COST

The PC requisition process discussed earlier dealt with one aspect of measuring process cost. In the example, we measured the labor cost of all the participants in the process. This was fairly easy to do since they were all employees of the company. Such cost information ordinarily is not collected or organized this way. Even so, the producer's costs are usually much easier to obtain than the customer's cost.

In Chapter 3, we discovered that many management reports are tabular in format (arranged in rows and columns) but that end-users tend to prefer graphics. A reason producers cite for not changing the format of such reports is the cost to produce these graphs. They may very well be able to show that the cost of producing a report will quadruple if it is created as a graph. This represents the process cost incurred by the producer.

However, if we consider the total cost of use—the process time all users incur to make sense of the report—it usually dwarfs the producer's cost. Where is cost of use addressed in your organization's internal and external product design standards?

Crosby and others talk about the cost of rework. Some groups have estimated that the cost to do things over can amount to 25 cents of a company's revenue dollar. This is a conservative estimate of the producer's cost.

Taguchi's quality loss function addresses the cost of poor quality to society. His statistical methods for measuring this are beyond the scope of this book. However, the importance of this concept is illustrated by one of his examples.

A firm manufactured a plastic film that farmers used to protect their crops. The company received a number of warranty claims due to the film's tendency to tear under windy conditions. The cost of warranty claims was easily measured, but the true loss to society (the broadest cost of use measure) was much larger and included the following:

- Lost crops and income for the user (farmer)
- Higher cost to consumers of remaining crops
- Loss of the farmer's productive growing season
- Loss incurred by other businesses because a greater percentage of consumer's disposable income had to be spent on more expensive food

Taguchi's concepts apply to the story earlier in this chapter about a company's problems getting PC requisitions processed in a timely manner. This problem seemed on the surface to be a common bureaucratic occurrence. The real source of the problem was the technology purchasing policy. The policy was a product created by a senior manager. We've already discussed the poor quality of the policy in terms of the approval criteria being a secret. It is well known that senior managers earn big bucks. What is not known is the cost to produce their products. If we as executive managers don't think about what we do as *creating products*, then it's no surprise that we don't measure either their cost or quality. We also do not measure the cost to society as a result of poor quality policies. If we did, these are some of the losses we would discover:

- Lost employee productivity due to trial and error attempts to figure out what management wanted in the requisition
- Lost competitiveness for the company due to lack of appropriate tools so its products could be first to market
- Loss of profit to the company
- Loss of jobs when positions had to be cut
- Loss of income to other businesses in the community that provided goods and services to previously employed citizens

The requisition/purchasing policy can be called a source product. Source products include strategies, plans, and policies. They are created by executive management. Source products are the directing influence on major corporate processes. Most source products are created exclusively for internal consumption. In the case of the requisition/purchasing policy, its immediate costs to use, once discovered, can provide a strong incentive to change our processes. I have long advocated that organizations give every budget-holding employee a checkbook or debit card with his/her piece of the annual budget in an account. Where versions of this approach have been used, employees are extremely frugal.

MEASURING YIELD AND BATCH

Anyone who has ever been a gardener understands yield. It is the result we get compared with our investment. The package of seeds we buy may list the germination rate as 85 percent. This means that if we plant 100 seeds, 85 will sprout. What the package doesn't say is how many pounds of vegetables or fruits each plant will produce. Both the germination rate and the pounds produced per plant are versions of yield. Germination rate is important because it indicates how close we should plant seeds, allowing for those which won't sprout. Pounds of produce created per plant influences how many plants we will need to cultivate. Some plants which sprout may not survive to harvest time. To improve our productivity, we must answer these questions:

- How many seeds of plant X must be sown to result in 100 pounds of produce?
- What is the cost per 100 pounds of produce?
- How can we raise the yield for the same cost?
- How can we reduce the cost for the same yield?

It is clear that yields in the garden change at different points in the growing process. Our challenge is to apply the same concepts to the information age and service processes.

The concept of yield certainly applies to the PC requisition process we've discussed. There is a common misperception that the results themselves represent yield. In other words, if we know that 50 requisitions were filled in the past quarter, we may assume that represents the yield of the process. Not necessarily. We could have initiated 500 requisitions. If 50 got filled, our yield is 50/500 or 10 percent. If we initiate 50 and have to recycle every one of them three times before we get them filled, do we still have 100 percent yield?

Our objective must be to achieve 100 percent yield on the first try, not through rework. This goal applies to every product created in the process, beginning with the source product. If all users of the requisitions policy and related procedures can complete a requisition that is accepted at the first review step, we have 100 percent yield up to that point in the process. If we have none returned for additional work at the second review step, we would again have 100 percent yield. Yield should be measured at each interim (or go/no go) point as well as at the end of the process.

Sales has the "15-5-1 rule," which states that of 15 possible buyers ("suspects"), 5 will be qualified as likely to buy ("prospects") and one will actually become a customer. The steps address the yield from suspect to prospect, prospect to customer, and suspect to customer. The yields in this process are 33.3 percent (5/15), 20 percent (1/5), and 6.6 percent (1/15), respectively. Table 6-3 illustrates the impact yields within the process have on the total process yield.

The most important observation is that the total process yield is never greater than the lowest yield at any interim point. This table illustrates several things. Doubling the number of suspects who become prospects without changing the number of customers obtained (rows E through G) achieves no advantage. The yield of C/P is called the close rate. Even if we can achieve the close rate of 60 percent shown in row C *and* the qualification rate of 66.6 percent shown in rows E through H, we still aren't very close to 100 percent yield for the whole process.

A final observation is that the point of lowest yield within the process is the target to work on first. Row D shows that even with a close rate of 100 percent, we can't get a total yield which is higher than the lowest internal yield, 33.3 percent.

The yield relationships are of great significance when looking at the impact of a source product on subsequent business processes.

Conclusion

The time consumption of a business process can be viewed from the perspectives of an internal producer and a customer. Setting a first-time improvement objective of 80 percent cycle time reduction experienced by customers is sufficiently dramatic to encourage rethinking of the whole way

Row	Number of Suspects (S)	Number of Prospects (P)	Number of Customers (C)	Qualification rate (yield of P/S)	Close rate (yield of C/P)	Process yield (yield of C/S)
A	15	5	1	33.3%	20%	6.6%
B	15	5	2	33.3%	40%	13.3%
C	15	5	3	33.3%	60%	20%
D	15	5	5	33.3%	100%	33.3%
E	15	10	1	66.6%	10%	6.6%
F	15	10	2	66.6%	20%	13.3%
G	15	10	3	66.6%	30%	20%
H	15	10	6	66.6%	60%	40%

Table 6-3: Impact of yields within process on total process.

we work. Once we cut how long things take (duration), then we can work on consistency (precision and certainty). The benefits include simplicity, reduced cost, higher yield, and better teamwork. The challenge is to *think* globally about the final products while acting locally with our own products and processes.

We must keep the final product, its customers, and customer expectations firmly in mind as the context and purpose for whatever we do with our own products and processes. This serves the dual purpose of preventing suboptimization (working on our own issues to the possible disadvantage of others) and keeping the focus on issues we can actually change (rather than trying to eliminate world hunger).

Your experience with these process exercises may be similar to those of our clients. Some of their discoveries have included the following:

- Most of our process activity is done serially or sequentially, not in parallel.
- We didn't believe 80 percent of the time could be cut until we used the FACT sheet; then we found that 80 percent reduction is conservative.

- Some of our current quality management policies and methods actually hurt cycle time.
- Inspections and reviews cause a lot of the process bottlenecks and delays.
- The earliest products created in the process should be redesigned to streamline our work.
- Our process measurements don't make us focus on what our customers want.
- There are redundant documents and activities.
- A lot of our delays can be cut by reducing the batch size, with the goal being a batch size of one (known as customization and just-in-time).
- Identifying the functions tells me who should be involved in a cross-functional team to work on this process.
- We need to use process mapping, VAT analysis for all processes.
- "Batch processing" is deeply imbedded in our systems.

Figure 6-6 illustrates two ways of directing change. A producer-centered culture will typically focus on improving internal processes to create products with wonderful capabilities for undifferentiated customers. This creates outcomes we don't know or can't measure. The long-term future is not attractive.

The customer-centered culture begins the improvement initiative by identifying the outcomes each type of customer expects. The expectations are translated into product design criteria, favoring end-users' needs. Process changes create the desired product so that ease of use, timeliness, certainty, and cost of ownership provide satisfaction for the customer and competitive advantage for the producer.

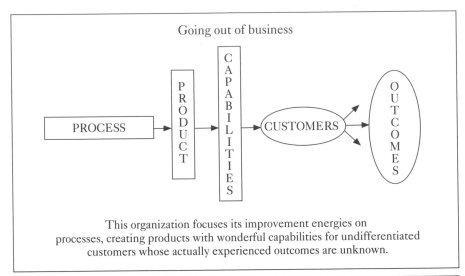

This organization focuses its improvement energies on
processes, creating products with wonderful capabilities for undifferentiated
customers whose actually experienced outcomes are unknown.

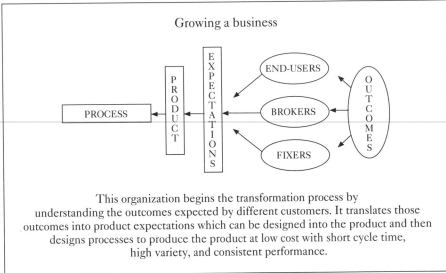

This organization begins the transformation process by
understanding the outcomes expected by different customers. It translates those
outcomes into product expectations which can be designed into the product and then
designs processes to produce the product at low cost with short cycle time,
high variety, and consistent performance.

Figure 6-6: Producer-centered thinking v. customer-centered thinking.

EXERCISE 7: PROCESS MAPPING WITH THE FACT SHEET

Objectives:
1. Describe the "as is " current activity flow in the process.
2. Prioritize opportunities to reduce time consumption.
3. Discover "should be" (if everything was done as specified) and "could be" (through innovations) solutions.

Using the fact sheet:
1. Name the final product the customer receives (the purpose of this process.)
2. Name the product/deliverable that is first created in this process.
3. Identify the event or condition that ends this process.
4. Identify the event or condition that begins this process.
   Note: Steps 3 and 4 define the scope of the process.
5. Estimate the elapsed cycle time, based on your experience, from the event described in 4 to the event described in 3.
6. In box 6a, write the name of the customer group which will receive the final product. Then, in boxes 6b through 6h, write the names of the organizational functions that are involved in this process.
7. a. Identify which function takes the first action.
   b. On a Post-it™ note, write that first activity as succinctly as possible. Start the statement with a verb and end it with a noun.
      Example: Requests product information.
   c. Then write in the upper left corner of the Post-it™ note, the estimated average work time (value-added time, or VAT) required for that activity, excluding any delays and waiting time. In the upper right corner, record the average elapsed (cycle) time for this activity. VAT is normally in terms of minutes; cycle time is stated in terms of days. Remember, from the customer's perspective there are 24 hours in a day, 7 days in a week.
   d. Stick the Post-it™ note to the chart (or on a larger version/flip chart) on the left side of the appropriate row.
   e. Continue this process, as quickly as possible, for all activities. Placement of the Post-it™ notes should indicate the relative sequence of the activities over time. Only activities that occur simultaneously (in parallel) should be shown in a column. The flow of activity can be indicated with lines connecting the boxes.
8. Add up all the work time represented by the activity boxes (VAT) in each row and record this total at the end of each row.
9. Add up the total for all rows. This is the VAT for this process.
10. Add up the cycle time for each row of activity boxes.
11. Add up the total for all rows. This is the total process cycle time.

Presentation:
1. Report answers to steps 1 through 5.
2. How many functions are involved in the process?
3. What percent of total cycle time is the VAT?
4. Where should you focus the first improvement effort(s)?
5. What are your discoveries?

Page ___ of ___ .

FACT SHEET Function, activity, and time

① Final product: _____
② Initial product: _____
③ Process ends when: _____
④ Process begins when: _____
⑤ How long does it presently take to go from 4 to 3? a. Best case ___ b. Worst case ___ c. Average ___

⑥ Function	⑦ Activity								⑧ VAT	⑩ Cycle
6a *Customer*										
6b										
6c										
6d										
6e										
6f										
6g										
6h										

Total VAT ⑨ _____ Minutes / Days ⑪

☐ Current   ☐ Proposed   Prepared by _____

FACT SHEET Function, activity, and time

Page ___ of ___ .

① Final product: ___
② Initial product: ___
③ Process ends when: ___
④ Process begins when: ___
⑤ How long does it presently take to go from 4 to 3? a. Best case ___ b. Worst case ___ c. Average ___

⑥ Function	⑦ Activity						⑧ VAT	⑩ Cycle
6a *Customer*								
6b								
6c								
6d								
6e								
6f								
6g								
6h								
⑨ Total VAT							Minutes	Days
								⑪

☐ Current   ☐ Proposed   Prepared by ___

EXERCISE 8: PRODUCT–ROLES MATRIX

Objectives:
1. Describe the "as is " activity flow in the process.
2. Identify the producers and end-users of each product.
3. Prioritize opportunities to:
   • Reduce time consumption
   • Eliminate or consolidate products
   • Enhance seamless flow
   • Clarify process and product purpose and ownership
4. Recommend action.

Using the product-roles matrix:
1. Identify the products in this process.
   a. Name the *target product*. It is the final product created by this process. It is the purpose of the process.
   b. Identify the *intermediate products* that are currently required to create the target product. Brainstorm and list all the intermediate products (documents, deliverables, parts, and so on) that are used during the process. Refer to the activities described on the FACT sheet to help you with this step.
   c. Name the *source products* (policies, strategies, or plans) that describe the intent or purpose of the process. Write the names of those specific documents here. Who produces them? If there is currently no source product, write "none."
2. Identify the *producer* for each product.
3. Name the *end-users*. These are the customers who will use the product to achieve some desired outcome.
4. Indicate the sequence in which the products first occur in the process; 1 = first product.
5. What actions should you take? _____
   _____
   _____
   _____
   _____

6. What discoveries did you make? _____
   _____
   _____
   _____
   _____

	① Products	② Producers	③ End-users	④
① Source				
① Intermediate				Sequence
① Target				

7

Implementation

[T]here is nothing more difficult to carry out, nor more doubtful of success, nor more dangerous to handle, than to initiate a new order of things. For the reformer has enemies in all those who profit by the old order, and only lukewarm defenders in all those who would profit by the new order; this lukewarmness arising partly from fear of their adversaries, who have the laws in their favour; and partly from the incredulity of mankind, who do not truly believe in anything new until they have had actual experience of it. Thus it arises that on every opportunity for attacking the reformer, his opponents do so with the zeal of partisans, the others only defend him half-heartedly, so that between them he runs great danger.*

Niccolo Machiavelli, *The Prince*

The blunt truth is that change agents wear targets on their bodies. The personal risk can be both exhilarating and stressful. The promise of success makes the risk worthwhile.

The dual purposes of this chapter are to help minimize risk to both you and your organization and to maximize successful results. Whether you are at the top of your organization or somewhere else within it, we'll discuss what you can do personally to guide the cultural transformation process.

*© 1952 by The New American Library of World Literature, Inc. Reprinted by permission of Oxford University Press.

An organization's culture is based on commonly shared language, beliefs, values, relationships, and behaviors. It cannot be changed overnight. We can increase the rate of cultural change by simultaneously targeting each of these elements of the cultural foundation. Top management is in the best position to do this. It controls the institutions and cultural systems. This is why its active involvement in (not just commitment to) the change process is critical to sustainable success. On the other hand, guerrilla warfare can be highly effective in obtaining both top management involvement and fast, focused successes. This chapter will address strategy that is effective for both the frontal assault and guerrilla warfare approaches to change.

This book began with a focus on language because it is so central to culture. Understanding the meaning of words like *service, product,* and *customer* enabled further examination of relationships (especially regarding power) and values (revealed by what you measure and reward). Your mastery of these concepts, applied to your own work, is essential to implement the strategies, structure, and process for getting from where you are to where you want to be.

STRATEGIES FOR CHANGE

Past successes offer insight into creating rapid and dramatic customer-centered change, while understanding why previous change efforts have failed can at least keep us from making the same mistakes again. Let's first discuss what has not worked and why. See Figure 7-1 for some of the reasons change initiatives fail.

There are four major organizational strategies in use aimed at improving quality and productivity. All have made contributions and continue to have value but also have inherent weaknesses which limits their effectiveness.

Problem-Driven Change

One example of the problem-driven change strategy was popularized by Crosby under the name zero defects. Crosby convinced managers that it is possible to have perfect products. That idea was a paradigm buster at the time. Another Crosby contribution was to put the concept of quality into a form management could understand. He showed how to quantify the costs incurred by making poor quality products. This *cost of*

1. The initiative's purpose is ambiguous and/or not agreed to by the involved parties.

2. The concepts and methods are not personally relevant to and/or practiced by management.

3. The overall conceptual framework supporting the initiative is either absent or inadequate.

4. The scope, pace, and manner of deployment are inappropriate for the results expected.

5. The tools provided are inappropriate or insufficient.

6. Activity is treated as an end in itself.

7. The relationship of the initiative to the business plan and organizational objectives is weak.

8. Strategic business priorities, measures, and incentives fail to support, or are in conflict with, the initiative.

9. Successes do not have a clear impact on improving customers' experience or competitive position.

10. The current improvement effort is perceived as the best and final solution.

Figure 7-1: Why change initiatives fail.

quality represented significant financial opportunity. He made quality personally relevant to management.

There are at least two unfortunate aspects of the zero defects concept. The first is that building a perfect and low-cost buggy whip does not ensure survival. Second, while it is admirable to seek out and eliminate problems continually, there are *so many* problems. The challenge is to either live long enough to solve all the problems or find a method for identifying which problems to tackle first. Reasons 1, 4, 5, and 6 in Figure 7-1 apply to the limited success of these initiatives. Problem-driven change can be habit-forming without necessarily moving to a proactive approach.

One purpose of employee suggestion programs is to put everyone to work finding problems and recommending solutions. Toyota is an example of a company that has fully integrated a suggestion collection and response system into its culture. Toyota employees generate tens of thousands of suggestions per year, and most are implemented. There is no question that widespread problem-solving contributes to Toyota's leadership position. Achieving Toyota's level of participation and success has required new roles for managers, a different way of thinking about the contribution potential of employees, and excellent follow-through.

Problem-driven change efforts by American organizations have not been so well organized. Problem solving tends to be a reactive, ad hoc activity aimed at the wheels that squeak most loudly. Routinely I am asked by managers and project team members how to select the "right" problems to address in a sea of problems. The answer to that question provides one of the keys to sustainable success.

Even though problem-driven change has its weaknesses, it has been the starting point for all the Malcolm Baldrige National Quality Award winners through 1991. Identifying life-threatening problems is sometimes the only strategy that is compelling enough to create radical change. More than a few executives have told me that their organizations don't need to do anything more about quality, innovation, or speed because they are already successful. There is nothing like a major disaster to transform arrogant disinterest into receptiveness to new ways. Once there is receptiveness, we have to make sure the problems addressed first are the ones that will have the highest impact on customer satisfaction and organizational performance.

Team-Driven Change

Teams are often a vehicle for problem-driven change, though their stated purpose may be to foster participation. Quality circles were popular in the United States during the early 1980s. Typically teams were composed of employees from the same work group. The model for these teams came from Juran's efforts in post-World War II Japan. Teams were initially created to disseminate problem-solving methods to a broad audience and to help build industrial capability.

The quality circle model adopted by many American companies failed due to almost all of the reasons shown in Figure 7-1. From the very beginning, there was conflict between quality circle proponents and traditional managers. Some proponents argued that the primary purpose of teams was to empower people to solve problems. Managers typically expected measurable cost savings. In fact, some management supporters mandated that a certain number of teams be created within a specific time frame. This quota-setting approach is characteristic of much management thinking. As late as 1990, one telecommunications company was besieged by grievances from its union employees because of forced participation on teams. Managers themselves did not usually participate as team members, and team methods and process had little personal relevance to a manager's daily work.

The scope of the typical quality circle was confined to issues the natural work group had authority to change. This constraint automatically eliminated the biggest improvement opportunities, which were cross-functional.

The quality circle movement made many contributions in spite of the barriers. Perhaps the biggest impact was to create awareness for empowerment and teamwork. The movement set the stage for the current push for high performance self-managed work teams.

SWAT teams and task forces are other vehicles for deploying problem-driven change. The benefit is that these efforts are usually highly focused, have clear management sponsorship, and develop action plans quickly. The flip side is that, when imposed upon others, recommendations may not be implemented in an effective and timely way. Recipients of proposed changes are often unreceptive when change is shoved down their throats.

Training-Driven Change

Training-driven change is perhaps the strategy most in vogue today. Deming has been a vocal proponent of training everyone in statistical methods.

Several years ago, a large international food company began a total quality initiative. Top management struggled to determine how the effort should be organized and who should direct it. The formal quality function had been around forever. Its focus was on compliance. The quality professionals had done little to generate excitement about the improvement potential to be gained from widespread use of their analytical tools. When top management began to hear about TQM, where everyone used certain techniques to make improvement, the idea didn't come from the quality professionals. Consequently, they were disqualified from the leadership role. Top management brought in external consultants to advise it, selecting a large consulting firm with expertise in manufacturing quality. That firm advised management to train all employees in process improvement and problem-solving tools.

Management realized that it was going to be expensive to train several thousand employees at headquarters, not to mention training employees in all of its plants. It was clear that TQM meant mass training. The corporate human resources department was enlisted to take over the

TQM program. A plan was drawn up to put a few hundred employees through the training each month.

Early results were mixed. Many people thought that although the concepts and tools of statistical process control and problem solving were interesting, they didn't apply to them personally. The concepts, language, and examples were oriented to manufacturing, not to knowledge and service work. Others got excited anyway about the possibility for improvement. They began to apply the training to their own work needs. As they came up against barriers, they went back to the human resources group for help. The human resources department wanted to help but couldn't. It was too busy training. It had also never used the concepts and tools on real issues outside of the classroom. Its expertise was limited.

Over a year into the TQM training, the program came to a halt. Dissatisfaction with lack of results, competing time commitments, and inadequate follow-up support caused management to reexamine the deployment plan. One result was that a number of people in the human resources department were fired. Almost six years after it had first begun, this company is again trying to reorganize a TQM initiative. As you can imagine, many are skeptical that success is possible. This was just one of numerous training-driven change strategies we've seen.

*It is possible and, in fact, fairly easy for an organization to go downhill and out of business making the wrong product or offering the wrong type of service, even though everyone in the organization performs with devotion, employing statistical methods and every other aid that can boost efficiency.**

When management identifies issues like quality, leadership, productivity, and competitiveness, which have strategic importance, training often is used to initiate change. The good side is that employees are provided with new skills. The downside is that only a tiny percent of those trained actually use what they've been given. There seems to be an assumption that providing people with hammers and saws will enable them to build a house. Without changed thinking, clear purpose, and sufficient support, we cannot expect knowledge or tools to create desired outcomes.

*Reprinted from *Quality, Productivity, and Competitive Position* by W. Edwards Deming by permission of MIT and W. Edwards Deming. Published by MIT, Center for Advanced Engineering Study, Cambridge, MA 02139. Copyright 1982 by W. Edwards Deming.

The huge cost of these mass training efforts is largely money down the drain if the skills aren't used. Training is effective when (1) each participant is receptive to personal change, (2) participants know what they are expected to do with the knowledge and skills being taught, (3) the training content is relevant to the participant's work context, and (4) there is sufficient follow-up and support to minimize roadblocks preventing application. This should not be news. Yet it is amazing how often quality training is conducted without attending to these requirements for success. Properly focused training, delivered on a just-in-time basis, can get close to 100 percent utilization.

Customer-Driven Change

If we could say one person was responsible for shifting the spotlight to customers, it would be Tom Peters. Whereas traditional change strategies focused on internal organizational needs or on a particular tool kit or guru, Peters took the position that anything and everything should be done to focus on satisfying customers. The power of the customer-driven change strategy starts with creating an unambiguous objective. Problem solving, teamwork, and training are not the objectives. They are simply some of the means to achieve customer satisfaction.

For people accustomed to procedures, authority, and control, Peters' "anything goes" approach to customer satisfaction can be both liberating and chaotic. Many organizations have adopted a succession of programs without getting tangible results. Peters may thrive on chaos, but many people prefer some organization to the chaos. Just as there are too many problems for the problem-solving strategy to be effective, there can be too many opportunities available to select those most likely to satisfy customers. The challenge is to organize the opportunities to have maximum impact and make rapid organizational change as digestible as possible. The customer-centered culture strategy integrates the strongest features of teamwork, problem solving, and just-in-time training.

A CUSTOMER-CENTERED CULTURE CHANGE STRATEGY AND PROCESS

In the early 1980s, it was easy to conclude that senior management was not committed to quality and customer satisfaction. One needed only to look at how little time was spent at the top of the organization talking about these issues to see their level of priority. Thankfully, today there is great interest in and commitment to these survival issues. Management increasingly focuses on how to guide the change process so that results are obtained, not on whether change should occur.

Organizational life would be so much more agreeable if change were easily prescribed and execution were linear. It doesn't quite work like that. Our challenge here is to describe the change process succinctly enough to make it palatable yet completely enough to make it understandable and practical. A description of the implementation process is provided in Figure 7-2.

---

1. *Assessment*: Determine top management's interest in and capability for improving organizational performance and customer satisfaction. Identify which executives will be the most active leaders.
2. *Awareness*: Introduce the customer-centered culture model, language, and strategy as globally as possible. This introduction should be brief and personally relevant to all recipients.
3a. *Demonstration*: Invite and organize a limited number of cross-functional product teams to begin implementation. Those who do not initially wish to participate should not be penalized. Projects must meet these criteria:
   • Projects have *high potential* to create significant impact on organizational performance and/or customer satisfaction.
   • Sponsors and team members have *high readiness* to participate in projects.
   • Project results—not activity—will have *high visibility*.
   • Tangible results will occur within 12 months.
3b. *Training*: Provide just-in-time skill training and unlimited support for first teams, sufficient to ensure visibly significant success.
4. *Promotion, expansion, and integration*: Widely promote all project successes. Use this context for communicating improvement objectives, deployment plans, and invitations for additional projects to be initiated.

   Establish a top management team to create a plan for broad deployment and to identify key source products for initial focus. Carefully consider the need for a transformation structure; prevent the growth of bureaucracy. Evaluate the impact of measures and incentives (intrinsic and extrinsic) to promote or prevent transformation.

   Align business policies, plans, measures, objectives, systems, and incentives with the cultural transformation imperatives.

Figure 7-2: Customer-centered culture implementation process.

PHASE 1: ASSESSMENT

The first phase in any large-scale organizational change is to determine what outcomes are to be obtained, who will have responsibility for what, and how prepared the leaders are to achieve success. Many organizations are using the Malcolm Baldrige National Quality Award Criteria (See Figure 7-3) as a

1. Leadership

2. Information and analysis

3. Strategic quality planning

4. Human resource utilization

5. Quality assurance of products and services

6. Quality results

7. Customer satisfaction

(For detailed information on this topic, contact the American Society for Quality Control at 800-248-1946.)

Figure 7-3: Malcolm Baldrige National Quality Award criteria.

basis for self-assessment. The seven categories covered provide an excellent starting point to begin dialogue about organizational strengths and weaknesses. The criteria do not provide numerical improvement objectives nor methods for achieving them.

Management must set objectives for quality and customer satisfaction improvement, just as it does for revenue and volume. The Baldrige criteria only identify topics to be addressed. Many organizations' quality initiatives identify process improvement as an objective without specifying what aspects of process are to be improved and by how much. Without numerical objectives, any improvement becomes acceptable.

The objectives should primarily address expected results, *not* activity. The objectives that are set reveal the aggressiveness of management's vision and the level of commitment to change. For example, an organization's management can clearly convey its intent for major change by setting objectives like the following:

- Cut the number of customer defections by 30 percent per year for the next three years.
- Reduce cycle times on selected processes by at least 80 percent within the next 12 months.

- Achieve customer satisfaction of at least 97 percent with selected products.
- Double the number of customer referrals.

These objectives are not trivial, but they are achievable. One of the requirements of setting such objectives is that the "as is" situation must be understood before the objectives can be achieved. Establishing baselines requires that measurement be developed on issues that may not have been scrutinized previously. We are definitely not advocating that aggressive objectives be pulled from the air; but they must be sufficiently challenging to convey management's intent to run the business differently.

A quality executive in one of our client organizations initially rejected the notion of setting an objective of 80 percent cycle time reduction. She was an avid Deming fan and declared that setting this kind of objective was exactly the type of thing Deming cautioned management not to do. Her view was that Deming abhors all objectives, advocates process stability, and believes that only by changing the system could one achieve such change. In spite of her objections, every team that accepted the challenge consistently cut cycle times by at least 80 percent.

Changing the system is precisely what we are advocating—and not by little tweaks nor by exhortation. Leadership requires rethinking and redesigning what we do and how we do it. The first phase in the frontal assault on the status quo is to assess where we are and where we could be. If we look in the mirror and don't like what we see but are ready to make significant change, there *is* a future and we can proceed to phase 2. If we don't like what we see in the mirror but are not ready to change, guerrilla warfare and skunkworks efforts by others will have to suffice in the short term.

It is rare that all top managers in an organization are equally ready and able to lead the transformation process. A sufficiently probing assessment will uncover the initial leaders. The person's position or rank in the structure has little to do with this readiness to lead.

PHASE 2: AWARENESS

The second phase in the strategy is to provide awareness of the main concepts covered in this book. Those include the definition of knowledge/service work as tangible products, differentiation of customers into the three roles they play, determining what customers want, how to design for those wants, knowing how to streamline processes for speed and simplicity, and what to measure. Awareness and education should be provided to as much of the organization as possible and as briefly as necessary to achieve understanding. The purpose is to provide sufficient information to create interest in going to the next phase. The education can occur through self-study, interactive presentation, or workshops. We need to understand clearly the difference between education (conducted in this stage) and training (to be conducted later). To understand this difference, consider your teenager enrolled in sex *education*…and how you would feel if it were *training*. Experience strongly recommends global education but just-in-time training.

PHASE 3: DEMONSTRATION AND TRAINING

The third phase in the customer-centered culture strategy involves selecting and implementing demonstration projects. In the education phase, we need to clearly communicate that not everyone is expected to implement these concepts right away. Those who initially choose not to implement are in no way penalized. On the contrary, only a relatively few interested in implementation will be given the full support of the organization's limited resources. Those few must select target products (either internally or externally directed) for focus (see Figure 7-4). The selection of a product automatically determines which problems are addressed. In other words, problems are grouped by product. *The product is the basis for organizing a team-based project.* The organization's resources to be provided include specific training only for those teams that need it, at the time it is needed. Each project to be supported must meet three conditions for success.

The first condition for success is *high potential*. This refers to the potential of the project to have a significant impact on the performance of the business and/or customer (internal or external) satisfaction. Moving the copying machine from one place to another does not have high potential.

Products that are created early in the relationship with external customers often are excellent candidates for high potential projects. One such product is a customer order. This document usually is created by a salesperson and given to the first group in the order fulfillment process. One of our clients was a graphic arts business. Its sales organization had never designed the customer order to ensure that the customer's expectations were fully described or that the needs of order entry, scheduling, and production functions were considered. Eighty percent of subsequent problems

---

The "right" products include those that are:

• Possible for the organization to change

• Created earliest in the relationship with customers (internal or external)

• Most influential in the capture, retention, or defection of end-user customers

• Central to the mission (of the enterprise, function, department, or individual)

• Upstream in a process

• Vital to work performed by others

• Greatest time consumers

• Sources of error, complexity, cost, or dissatisfaction

Figure 7-4: Selecting products for high potential projects.

related to accuracy, timeliness, cost, and rework of the graphic product were caused by problems with the order.

A version of the customer order in the travel and hospitality industry is the reservation for a flight, hotel room, or restaurant. Customers are rarely asked about their special needs and preferences when they make a reservation. When was the last time the airline asked about your meal preference? A focus on the customer order can prevent problems and provide the basis for delighting customers.

Product designs and specifications are also products that can have high potential impact. Management information services and product engineering groups are notorious for creating designs that inadequately address the constraints and needs of those who will construct the final product.

In general, high potential projects can be found by focusing on products created at the front end of any business process. Exercise 9 at the end of this chapter provides a structured approach to selecting the products that best fit the criteria for high potential projects.

The second condition for the success of the project is *high readiness*. This refers to the receptiveness of individuals to change. Accept the fact that people in any organization will differ in readiness. Use this knowledge to guide the selection of projects, sponsors, and project team members.

Lack of intrinsic motivation to participate in a change initiative is possibly the greatest single cause of project failure. It is fairly easy to identify readiness. Someone who focuses on all the reasons change cannot occur is probably not ready. For those who are ready, no obstacle is too great; for those who are not ready, any obstacle is too great.

One way to augment readiness and success when starting the cultural change process is to restrict access to it. Consider the recruitment slogan of the U.S. Marines: "We're looking for a few good men." It is just as critical to have the right people involved in your initial efforts as it is to choose the right products. Instead of encouraging everyone's involvement during the education phase, be selective. By limiting access, you will drive up demand for involvement. The fewer who are initially involved, the greater your ability to provide support and training for them. Every effort must be made to ensure that the pioneers are successful.

The traditional approach to quality initiatives sets quotas on how many projects, teams, process improvements, and so on must be under way by a certain time. This is the push system. The customer-centered culture strategy takes the reverse approach by limiting the number of efforts only to those that can be properly sustained. It uses the pull system. The initiative's leaders should specify the maximum (but not the minimum) number of projects that will be supported at the beginning. As success occurs and the capability of the organization to support additional projects grows, others can be invited to participate.

So far we have addressed implementation as if it were planned and initiated at the top of the organization. We could call this the frontal assault approach. When commitment and personal involvement exist at the top, the frontal assault is ideal. However, even in the absence of strong leadership at the top, change can be effective if these keys for success are applied. Project leaders and participants must simply use guerrilla warfare tactics. Such efforts are sometimes also referred to as skunkworks. In any case, a highly dedicated team with a clear focus on a specific product and outcome can initiate action without waiting for top management's readiness. These two approaches—frontal assault and guerrilla warfare—are not mutually exclusive. Consider how you can use both.

The third condition for success of projects is *high visibility* of the results (not necessarily the activity). This means that the successful completion of a project will be noticed by many others. We have found this element to have great impact on accelerating the pace of subsequent deployment of the change initiative throughout the organization. This approach is diametrically opposed to the conventional practice of promoting "the total quality plan." Promotion of the promise for change invariably raises expectations that are not satisfied. While it is important for management to communicate new directions and objectives, save the heavy promotion activity for results actually achieved. This builds credibility, assures recognition of those who contributed to the success, and reduces the perception that the initiative is just one more program that will go away in a year or two. Whatever "plan" is promoted after that point, it will rest on a proven foundation.

A CASE STUDY*

One of our clients provides a case study illustrating these early phases of implementing the customer-centered culture strategy. A major U.S. transportation company was bought out by new management in early 1989. One of the old guard replaced in the following year was the executive vice president for human resources. When "Jack," the new executive vice president, joined this 45,000-employee company in May 1990, one of his first actions was to change his title to executive vice president for customer satisfaction through people involvement. His personal mission was clear and there was to be no mistaking it. Jack brought a big blast of fresh ideas to his new position.

In our first meeting that July, Jack shared with me his vision and his experiences with TQM. I shared with him the customer-centered culture strategy that focused primarily on customers, not process. The concepts intrigued him. He was also interested because Motorola, one of our clients since 1987, had won the Baldrige Award and continues to use the strategy. We mapped out a short-term plan of attack to demonstrate these new concepts.

The first step in the plan was to create awareness about this new way of thinking about quality and running the business. Jack felt it best to start the effort in the human resources division. He had control over all the issues there and wanted to keep the risk of failure low but ensure that the pace of change was high. Awareness was achieved by having most of the managers

---

*Reprinted with permission from NATIONAL PRODUCTIVITY REVIEW, VIIN3 Summer 1992. Copyright 1992 by Executive Enterprises, Inc., 22 West 21st Street, New York, New York 10010-6904. All rights reserved.

and many other professionals from human resources attend the "C4" seminar, "Creating a Customer-Centered Culture.™"

The second step was to select carefully a few "products" on which to focus the change effort. Four were chosen. Each product was the basis for a cross-functional project team that was expected to last from 4 to 12 months. Team members were invited to participate on the basis of their involvement with each selected product and their completion of the C4 seminar. Three critical success factors were used in selecting the products: (1) high potential, (2) high readiness, and (3) high visibility of results.

The first team meetings were held in November. Each team began the process outlined in Figure 7-5.

By design there were typically five to eight people per team. We had found that as teams go beyond eight members, team performance drops. Just scheduling meetings when everyone can attend becomes an increasingly difficult challenge. Team members were those from the highest level possible who actually handled or used the product. In addition to the standing team members, each team had a sponsor and a project leader. The team sponsor was a person who had authority over the issue to be addressed. The level of the sponsor determined the scope of the project. One role of the project leader was to act as an apprentice to the team facilitator and learn the customer-centered culture philosophy, concepts, and methods sufficiently well so that he/she could be part of the propagation effort later.

One team's project focused on the first retirement check retirees received. The new CEO had been getting complaints from retirees that their first pension check wasn't received until two months after they had stopped work. The pension check team was formed, consisting of representatives from the seven functions involved in the retirement process.

The pension check team successfully completed its project and presented its proposal to executive management in June 1991. That proposal included a complete process redesign that reduced the cycle time by 80 percent (from 124 days to 24). This team's work set the benchmark for other teams that were beginning to be formed. Some of this team's results are summarized in Table 7-1 and Figure 7-6.

The pension check team made a number of interesting discoveries as it proceeded through the project. One of the most dramatic occurred during the team's second meeting, when members discussed the scope of the process that results in the first pension check. Instead of just considering the process as a sequence of activities, they also looked at the flow of products in that process as required by the Customer-Centered Culture

Phase	Step	Tools
Focusing for results	1. Prioritizing improvement opportunities to maximize return on investment	Product inventory Target product selection matrix
Organizing the project	2. Organizing the project and team	Process overview chart Project outcomes matrix Sponsor's charter Team mission statement
Designing the product for customer satisfaction	3. Determining customers' expectations	Customer roles matrix Customer survey Outcomes matrix
	4. (Re) Designing the product	Innovation table Customer expectations matrix Customer satisfaction measurement table Product features design table

First sponsor review meeting

Designing the process for speed	5. Evaluating source products	Source products matrix
	6. Identifying intermediate products	Product–roles matrix
	7. Mapping the process	FACT sheet Process flow chart
	8. Determining key success predictors and identifying problems	Success predictors table Problem analysis

Second sponsor review meeting

Taking action	9. Measuring customer satisfaction, product quality, and process performance	Measurement plan
	10. Developing an implementation plan	Implementation plan

Final presentation to sponsor

Figure 7-5: Customer satisfaction project plan.

Model™. The team's discussion identified the first product in the process as an annual report printed in early January that listed all employees who were going to turn 65 during the year. The purpose of the report was to notify the employee records department of prospective retirees who should receive retirement forms.

	Current process	Proposed process	Improvement
Total cycle time (best case)	124.5 days	24.5 days	80%
Total cycle time (worst case)	253 days	82 days	68%
Days to receive first check (from retirement date)	61	31	49%
Number of steps in process	202	121	40%
Number of players	10	7	30%
VAT (value-added time)	5 hours, 16 minutes	2 hours, 52 minutes	46%

Table 7-1: Comparison of current to proposed process (for a normal retirement).

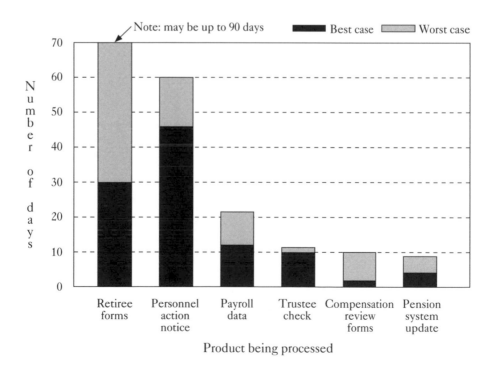

Figure 7-6: Product cycle in a current process for a normal retirement.

The experienced facilitator who lead the team asked what percent of the company's employees actually retired at age 65. The team responded that over 80 percent of retiring employees took early retirement. Depending on the type of employee and length of time employed, retirement could occur 5 to 10 years before age 65. The team had just made a key discovery: The first product in the process (the list of prospective retirees) was routinely created about *5 to 10 years late* for over 80 percent of employees. As the team later discovered, this was one of the reasons everyone involved in the process was constantly in a reactive mode. This problem was rapidly getting worse as the number of employees reaching early retirement age increased (see Figure 7-7).

What customers want is not
necessarily what they expect.

The pension check team made another set of discoveries when they conducted a focus group with recent retirees. While it was true that retirees

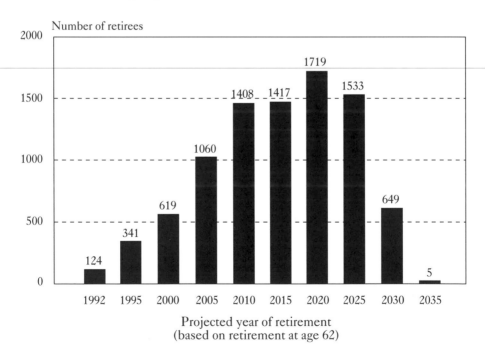

Figure 7-7: Retiree projections.

wanted to receive their first retirement check within a month of retiring, they had been told by the pensions department, prior to retirement, not to expect it for two months. The key discovery here is that what customers (retirees) want is not necessarily what they expect. Consequently, the timing of the first check actually ranked lower in retiree expectations than other things. This information enabled the pension check team to recommend significant changes in the way retirees were treated during the preretirement process. One retiree put it this way:

> *When I joined this company over 20 years ago, a lot of time was spent to welcome and orient me to my new job and the way things are done here. Retirement is a major life change. Nobody took such care to make sure I was as well prepared for this as for my first job. It would have made the transition easier and made me feel I was still valued.*

In spite of the third team's impressive results, its overall experience was pretty typical of other customer-centered culture projects we've conducted. A summary of its discoveries is shown in Table 7-2.

Team members were provided highly focused training on a just-in-time basis during the course of the project. This included the topics below, depending on the specific team needs. The pension check team received the training marked with asterisks.

- Conducting focus groups *
- Constructing surveys *
- Collecting, analyzing, and displaying data (affinity, cause-and-effect, Pareto, histogram, and scatter diagrams) *
- Mapping processes (Graham charting) *
- Making a compelling presentation *
- Time management (Time Systems)
- The house-of-quality matrices
- Measurement of time, yield, cost, and quality *
- Innovation
- Project management
- Team dynamics
- Statistical methods (DOE, SPC, ANOVA, and others)

Topic	Discoveries
Working as a team	• It was easier to identify problems that existed in someone else's department than in our own. • There are many things we do that defied explanation. • Acronyms and terminology specific to each department were barriers to communication. • Understanding of what "quality" meant was initially different for each team member but soon evolved to a consensus. • No one really had understood what anyone else did.
Customer needs	• Retirees actually received their first paycheck when they were supposed to, but they wanted to get it in half the time. • The top five priorities had nothing to do with timing of the first check. They were related to: –communication needs: right answer first time –pre-retirement information and forms –post-retirement benefits –desire for check stubs –state tax withholding
Products	• Everyone received all the forms, whether they needed them or not. • Forms were complicated to complete. • Nine pages of instructions were sent to each retiree to "help" them complete forms. • There were six major categories of forms. • One form is the single most important document that directs the whole process.
Process	• There was no documentation of the process. • The current process takes 124 to 253 days to create the first pension check, requiring 202 steps and involving eight departments. • Five hours and 15 minutes of work is spent on each retiree, about .05 percent of the total time.

Table 7-2: Discoveries of pension check team.

Many teams encounter a major obstacle to rapid project completion: insufficient time. They experience this in two ways. First, the project represents new work on top of an already overflowing plate of tasks. Today's lean organizations run chronically short of sufficient time just to do the existing work. Any project seeking to make major organizational change will compete with other priorities. Since most team members are not given a month or two off to do the project work, the reality of competing priorities must be addressed at the beginning of the project.

One of the responsibilities of the project's sponsor is to remove obstacles such as conflicting priorities from the path of team members. We have found that certain kinds of time management training can also be of great assistance in freeing participants from unproductive or disorganized work. An approach we find particularly effective is Time Systems. The half-day course and a special organizer help users integrate communications, projects, and tasks to gain an average of over four hours per week of productive personal time. Secondary benefits of this inexpensive program are that it offers a visible way to reinforce and model effective self-management and that it is personally relevant to the users. People who feel in better control of their day are more effective team players.

The second way time can be an obstacle is that team meetings are not of appropriate length. Teams that meet for only an hour per week are generally not very productive. Twenty-five to 50 percent of the hour can easily be consumed just in reviewing previous work and organizing future activity. We have found that meetings of two to four hours are ideal in most cases, with only 10 to 20 percent of the total time spent in reviewing and organizing. Figure 7-8 illustrates these relationships.

If personal time management is an issue, it must be dealt with as soon as possible. The other training topics should be in sufficiently modular form that bite-sized pieces are available to the team when needed. This pull system for training is not always an easy adjustment for the training organization to make, but it is consistent with changing the culture to be customer-responsive.

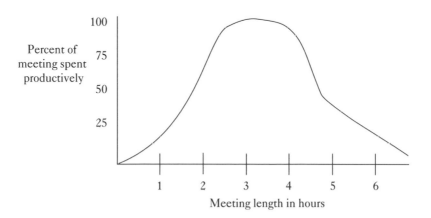

Figure 7-8: Meeting time and productivity.

The pension check team's presentation to executive management was videotaped in preparation to begin phase four of the implementation process. The video was included in communication throughout the organization to promote the early team successes, discuss the strategy for organizational transformation, and invite others to participate.

PHASE 4: PROMOTION, EXPANSION, AND INTEGRATION

The purpose of this phase is to model the desired behavior and accelerate the transformation. This should in no way be viewed as a requirement to reorganize the existing structure. That may come later through natural forces, but not now.

> *We trained hard...but it seemed that every time we were beginning to form up into teams, we would be reorganized. I was to learn later in life that we tend to meet any new situation by reorganizing; and a wonderful method it can be for creating the illusion of progress while producing confusion, inefficiency, and demoralization of our subordinates.*
>
> Petronious Arbiter, Grecian Navy, 210 B.C.

Petronious Arbiter's observation is as relevant today as it was 2,000 years ago. Especially in larger organizations, the push for quality has often been accompanied by additional bureaucracy. The desire to increase participative and consensus management can spawn committees and governing bodies that succeed only in slowing the pace of the transformation.

One place to model the desired behavior is with the formation of a management steering committee. Such groups are often established with the honorable intention of guiding the priorities and overall deployment process of the change initiative. One of the first breakdowns in this intent occurs by including all of the top managers on the steering committee. The sole criterion for membership is rank or position. If all top managers are equally "ready" to lead the change initiative through personal action, then it is reasonable to include them, but rarely is this the case. Some are more ready than others. There are three simple qualifications for steering committee membership. The prospective member must (1) presently be sponsoring, (2) be committed to begin sponsoring (within the next 60 days), or

(3) have sponsored to successful conclusion a project team demonstrating the values, concepts, and methods of the initiative on an important customer/business issue.

This criterion can prevent the steering committee from being a cozy club based on rank. It creates an elite powerhouse of movers and shakers. As with any high-performance team, limit the size to eight members. Heterogeneity in membership (in terms of rank, function, and expertise) builds in a reality base. For this to work well, titles must be treated as irrelevant as much as possible. If we want empowerment, this is a sure way to demonstrate it.

Resist the temptation to create an elaborate and separate structure for administering the transformation process. Florida Power and Light (FPL) offers an example of one organization where the passion for quality resulted in a bureaucratic nightmare. The growing complaints of managers and employees inundated by quality programs, meetings, and reporting finally caused FPL's top executives to dismantle the bloated quality function.

If and when reorganization is required, look for ways to integrate customer-centered thinking, behavior, and measurement into the lateral business flow. Organize horizontally, with the focus on key products.

Beginning the implementation process calls for careful selection of the right products, people, and improvement objectives. The intent is to stack the deck in our favor to ensure success. Once success has been demonstrated, an internal expertise base becomes established, and learning can be woven back into the replication process. We are then ready to open the throttle on the change process. Restricted access to new ways of doing business should, as quickly as possible, give way to expanded involvement and participation on a universal basis. "Quickly" is not necessarily measured in months. As an example, Motorola began its broad quality initiatives over 10 years ago. Great progress has been made, but most executives would admit there is still much to do. The pace of integrating the new concepts into daily application has rapidly increased within the last few years. It has come from relentless promotion of success, constant scrutiny of "the way we do things," and change in measurement to support the organizational vision of total customer satisfaction. Significant efforts are made to apply learning so the transformation accelerates. A worldwide, 100,000-employee organization doesn't turn on a dime. Yours won't either. The more you initially focus on the right things, involve the right people, and demonstrate meaningful results, the sooner the transformation will occur.

Conclusion

I have a strong personal bias for action that creates tangible results. If your desire is also for results, use the simple two-to-one rule for either the design of your quality leadership strategy or the evaluation of initiatives and programs already in place. Demand *at least* a two-to-one return on investment during the first three years of implementation. Quantifiable results less than this tell you that either the focus is not on the right issues, that the change initiative is not sufficiently effective, or that the measures are not in place to capture the return on investment.

It is true that many positive results should occur that won't or can't be measured. That's fine, as long as they are in addition to the two-to-one return on investment rule, not instead of it.

EXERCISE 9: TARGET PRODUCT SELECTION

Instructions:
1. Create a product inventory by listing in column 1, all the products produced by the organization on which you are focused. Consider the following figure.

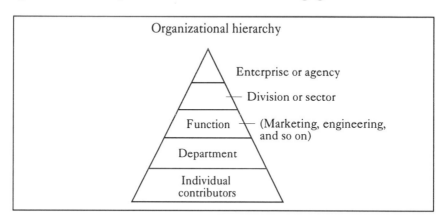

We recommend you begin the product inventory at the department or function level. Products that are created by cross-functional groups tend to offer the greatest potential improvement impact for the enterprise while being manageable to execute.

2. a.   Put a check in criteria column A next to each product that meets this selection criteria. Discard from further consideration any product for which change is not believed to be possible.

    b.   For criteria columns B through H, rank the top five products that *best* meet each criteria. For example, if 30 products are identified, the top five best meeting a specific criteria would be ranked 30, 29, 28, 27, and 26, respectively.

3. Total the score for each product.

4. Identify which five products have the highest scores. Rank the top five products in terms of their likelihood to have *high potential* for increasing both customer satisfaction and organizational performance (for instance, profit, cost, productivity, and cycle time).

5. Now consider the people who will need to sponsor and participate in a project addressing these priority products. For which product(s) are people *most ready* to engage in the change process?

TARGET PRODUCT SELECTION

	② Criteria "The right product is…"								③	④
Selecting the "right" product for your team	A	B	C	D	E	F	G	H		
	Possible for the organization to change	Created earliest in the relationship with customers	Most influential in the capture, retention, or defection of end users	Central to the mission	Vital to work performed by others	Greatest time consumer	Source of error, complexity, cost, or dissatisfaction	Upstream in a process		
① Products									Total	Rank
1										
2										
3										
4										
5										
6										
7										
8										
9										
10										
11										
12										
13										
14										
15										

8

Summary

This book has been intended to help you and your colleagues to think like your customers and then to take focused action to delight them and significantly strengthen your leadership position (both organizationally and personally). There are many concepts and principles included here whose meaning may require more than one reading to understand fully.

As stressed in the Introduction, the maximum value of this material can only be obtained by applying the exercises in each chapter and subsequently reflecting on and discussing your discoveries with others. Through many years of effort, I have found that the intellectual understanding of these concepts is no substitute for experiential learning. This is why so much emphasis has been placed on personalizing the principles and application of a few tools. It provides the basis for transferring the learning to unlimited applications.

We set out to answer five deceptively simple questions. They and their abbreviated answers are shown in Table 8-1.

Answering these questions required you to confront your current organization's value system. The value system is manifested by how we describe what we do, who we try to please, what we measure, and the objectives of our improvement efforts. Figures 8-1 and 8-2 contrast the values and priorities of producer-centered and customer-centered cultures.

These are presented as if the two cultural styles were at different ends of a spectrum. If you can determine which characteristics most closely

KEY QUESTIONS	ANSWERS
1. *What* do we do?	We create products.
2. *Who* do we do it for?	It should be for end-users but may actually be for brokers and producers.
3. What do they *want*?	Ease of use, timeliness, and certainty of products which best achieve the customers' desired outcomes.
4. How can we *improve*… • their satisfaction? • our performance?	Collect and organize customer expectations, measure the degree to which they get what they want, use continuous improvement on today's product, and use innovation to develop new products. Drastically cut process cycle time.
5. What is the *strategy* and *process* for creating a customer-centered culture?	Identify the products with highest potential to improve both customer satisfaction and organizational performance; identify people with greatest readiness to become leaders; provide active support and just-in-time training; and ensure that results to be obtained will be highly visible. Encourage change leaders to set aggressive, quantifiable improvement objectives to promote divergent thinking.

Table 8-1: Answers to five key questions.

match your own organization, you know how close you are to having a customer-centered culture.

The role of management is to demonstrate that we care about satisfying customers of the products we personally create, including policies, strategies, and plans. One of our biggest management challenges is to confront continually the vital lies that stifle change and innovative thinking. Divergent thinkers are often labeled "loose cannons," yet these loose cannons have been known to become entrepreneurial competitors. We need to create an environment in which they can be our allies, not our adversaries. The keys to our past successes are not necessarily the keys to a successful future.

A bright future will require our marketing and sales functions to take an active leadership role in directing successful quality/customer satisfaction

	Priorities of a producer-centered culture:	Priorities of a customer-centered culture:
	• System needs • Assets as money • Maintenance • Control • Tasks/process • Technical • Problem solving rewarded • Internal focus	• Customer needs • Assets as people • Experimentation • Empowering • Outcome/satisfaction • Perception and performance • Problem prevention (design) rewarded • External focus

Figure 8-1: Cultural priorities.

	Producer-centered culture	Customer-centered culture
Power and relationships	• Product design and development is the exclusive domain of the producer. • Brokers represent producers' interests and encourage users to accept the product. • Fixers have little influence on either product or process changes and usually function in a reactive mode.	• Product design is done collaboratively with intended users. • Brokers represent the customer and work with the producer to meet continuously changing needs. • Fixers solicit input from users and work with brokers and producers to improve the product's design and performance.
Values	• Producers cater to internal needs of the system. • Money is viewed as the most important asset. • Most organizational energy is devoted to maintenance, control, and problem solving. • Service product quality is based on technical performance against accepted industry standards.	• Producers focus on meeting customers' needs. • People, both employees and customers, are viewed as most important. • Special emphasis is given to supporting experimentation and rewarding creativity. • Both product performance and its perception by customers are considered in assessing level of quality.

Figure 8-2: Comparison of two cultural styles.

initiatives. This is a change many organizations have yet to make. In fact, my observation has been that the sales and marketing folks are rarely involved in these initiatives. How can we be customer-centered without them? When sales and marketing are directing the entire customer satisfaction and total quality leadership efforts of the enterprise, we know we have finally completed the transformation that began in the first half of the twentieth century. Deming, Ishikawa, and others said we can't input quality into our products after we build them. They advocated focusing on the process to be more proactive. The ultimate revolution in thinking is accomplished when we start creating customer satisfaction in the product development phase, heavily influenced by the work of marketing and sales and by customers.

Global and domestic competition are likely to increase. It is a race that doesn't end, except for those who can't or won't play. Consider it akin to a horse race. The cost to own a racehorse can range from as little as a few thousand dollars to as much as several million. There is large variation in the price required just to be in the game. But consider the difference between the horse that wins and the one that finishes second. The difference in performance is about 2 percent. I hope this book helps you achieve that 2 percent edge. Good luck!

Appendix: Questions and Answers

The following represent some of the most frequently asked questions. We know this book may not answer all your questions. We are prepared to fill any gaps or just hear your comments. Please send your questions or comments to us at the address below. Include a stamped, self-addressed business envelope, along with your title, daytime phone number, and fax number (if available).

Questions should be addressed to:
International Management Technologies, Inc.
E-mail: imt@imtc3.com
http://www.imtc3.com
Fax: (612) 953-6928

Q. Isn't my boss my most important customer?

A. Not necessarily. This question carries an implied threat: If my boss isn't happy with me, I could be replaced. It is always important to satisfy those on whom we depend. However, we can depend on the boss without the boss being a customer. The customer role is always determined by a specific product. If your boss has asked you for a report on a certain topic, then the boss is your customer regarding the report. What type of customer he/she is depends on the reason the boss will receive the report. The options are as follows:

Purpose	Role
1. to use it to achieve a desired result	end-user
2. to pass it to someone else who will use it	broker
3. to approve it	inspector
4. to modify or correct it for the benefit of an end-user	fixer

Q. Is "client" the same as "customer"?

A. The terms are usually synonymous. Just as customers can be differentiated by their roles with a product (end-users, brokers, and fixers), so can clients. Each industry or profession uses "client" uniquely. In human services and health care, client can mean the same as patient; it can reveal power roles. In business services like accounting, consulting, and advertising, client can refer to the organizational entity being served. Some people speak of clients as those organizations and individuals with whom they have an ongoing relationship, while customers are viewed as those with whom they have a limited number of transactions. I see no practical difference between client and customer. Just be sure to know who the end-users of your products are.

Q. Can a person or group have more than one role with a product?

A. Certainly. Small business managers are traditionally known to "wear many hats." Most of us do this too, under differing circumstances. View the hats as roles. Such a person can be a producer, broker, and fixer. Even though this role mix is common, there is usually one role that consumes the most time or has the main priority. Remember that roles are always defined in relation to a specific product.

Q. Is it better to focus on performance or perception attributes of a product?

A. Ask your end-user customers.

Q. Why is it important to focus on a product's "functional" attributes first, rather than features or "content" attributes?

A. The functional attributes represent the voice of the customer: the customer's statements of desires for the product. When we begin thinking of the product at this level, we assure the broadest inclusion of customer expectations. It encourages divergent thinking. If we skip this step and go directly to content attributes, we're likely to reinforce our natural convergent thinking and miss breakthrough potential. It is much easier for producers and customers to come up with ideas for new features than to rethink alternatives to an existing product.

Q. Is knowledge a product?
A. No, it is either an outcome or a resource. Knowledge may be an outcome that the customer obtains by using products like courses, reports, articles, and so on. Knowledge can also be the resource or raw material used to create a product. Unless knowledge is packaged into discrete units, it is not a product.

Q. How do you get customers to tell you what they want?
A. The short answer: Ask them. Interviews, focus groups, and surveys are three common methods of asking. I strongly recommend interviews and focus groups instead of surveys, for several important reasons. Of primary importance is that both interviews and focus groups can provide rich qualitative information about customer expectations that cannot be collected in the highly structured survey approach. No matter what approach is used, the wrong questions asked the wrong way of the wrong people will yield information of dubious value at best and harmful information (for the producer who acts on it) at worst. If you could ask a customer only four questions, the following are what I recommend, in the order shown. Assume you are interested in designing or improving a manual.

1. A satisfying manual is one that *results in* what?
2. For what are you going to use this manual?
3. A manual is one that *is* what?
4. A manual is one that *has* what?
   Questions 1 and 2 will identify expected outcomes. Questions 3 and 4 will reveal expected product functions and features, respectively.

Q. **You put almost exclusive emphasis on satisfying end-users. Aren't the other customers important, too?**

A. All customers are important and our goal must be to satisfy them all. In real life, I have observed that producers of both internally and externally consumed products consistently favor the interests of brokers over end-users and fixers. This situation is less a matter of making a conscious decision than a matter of default. There are several reasons that this occurs:

- Producers may be confused about who the end-users of a product are. Differentiation of customers into the end-user, brokers, and fixer roles can solve this problem.
- Producers may not have direct contact with the end-users.
- Customers can have competing interests. Producers often choose to satisfy certain expectations over others, based on the power of the competing customers. A customer's relative power flows from four common characteristics:
  - position (level of person in an organization's structure)
  - purse strings (those who are perceived to have the money get preferential treatment)
  - proximity (those who are closest to, or have the most contact with, the producer)
  - personality (those with the most personal persuasiveness)

These characteristics are often those of brokers, not end-users. My emphasis on satisfying end-users is intended to counteract possible short-term thinking on the part of producers and encourage them to do those things that will enhance their leadership position. End-users always win in the long run.

Glossary

Attribute
A characteristic of a product, process, or outcome. All attributes are measurable. Performance attributes describe objective criteria; perception attributes describe subjective criteria.

Broker
A customer who acts as an agent of the end-user and/or the producer. As an *agent of the end-user*, the broker makes the product more accessible, easier to use, and more appealing. As an *agent of the producer*, the broker "encourages" the user to accept the product.

Certainty
A category of attributes that includes accuracy, reliability, predictability, and consistency.

Culture
An organization's culture reflects commonly shared language, beliefs, values, relationships, and behaviors. Whether a culture is producer-centered or customer-centered depends on whose needs primarily direct the development, creation, and modification of products. The measures used to manage the organization reveal the culture's priorities.

Customer

Any individual or function who receives a product to achieve a desired outcome (end-user); transfers the product to someone else (broker); or transforms, repairs, corrects, or modifies it (fixer). A customer's role is always determined by a specific product. A customer role may change if the product changes. A customer can have more than one role simultaneously.

Cycle Time

The total elapsed time or duration of a process, usually measured in days; it includes value-added time, delays, inspections, and rework.

End-User

The customer for whom the product is primarily intended. This customer will personally use the product to achieve a desired outcome. There are usually more customers of this type than of any other. This is the most important type of customer.

Expectations

Customer expectations are the basis for determining what "quality" means. Customers have expectations about the performance and perception attributes of the product as well as the outcomes to be achieved by using the product. These expectations are stated in the "voice of the customer," which may not be directly measurable. They have to be translated by the producer into precise design criteria, which are directly measurable. Producers sometimes refer to these translations as *requirements*, *specifications*, *needs*, or *standards*. None of these terms are as inclusive as expectations; they reflect the minimum to be achieved by the product and generally are focused on performance attributes.

Fixer

Any customer who will have to make repairs, corrections, modifications, or adjustments to the product at any point in its life cycle for the benefit of the end-user.

Innovation

The process of making a desired outcome easier to achieve.

Inspector

Someone who approves others' work.

Nominal Measure
Counts of things, organized by category.

Ordinal Measure
A measure reflecting rank, priority, sequence, or rating scale.

Outcome
The results achieved by using the product.

Power
The ability to direct or change the product design.

Process
The sequence of activities and events that creates the product. Usually, many processes contribute to the creation of a single product.
Also:
The flow of products whose final product is intended to create desired outcomes for the end-user customer.

Process Owner
Primary person or group responsible for the performance of the process, the internal resources used in the process, and the satisfaction of the customers who use the product produced.

Producer
Person or group responsible for making a product that meets customer expectations.

Product
A deliverable created as a result of work activity. It is:

- a noun
- countable
- a unit of output that is given to a customer
- packaged information that occurs in discrete units
- expressed as something that can be made plural (with an s)

Quality
The degree to which a product meets customer expectations.

Relationship Measure
A measure of correlation, prediction, or regression. Also, a ratio.

Requirement
See **Expectations.**

Source Products
Source products include strategies, plans, and policies. They are produced by management. Source products are the directing influence on major corporate processes. They define the purpose or intent of the process. Most source products are created exclusively for internal consumption.

Substitute Quality Characteristic (SQC)
An SQC consists of two parts: a unit of measure and a performance attribute of the product or process that is directly measurable. SQCs transform the voice of the customer (VOC) into design criteria for both products and processes.

Value-Added Time (VAT)
Time consumed or expended in performing work, usually measured in minutes. For many business processes, VAT accounts for .05 to 5 percent of the total process cycle time.

Variation Measure
A measure such as range, standard deviation, or variance. Six sigma is an example of a variation measure used as a goal by some organizations.

Vital Lie
A term coined by playwright Henrik Ibsen and used as justification (often unfounded or inappropriate) for current practices or beliefs.

Voice of the Customer (VOC)
Expectations of the product, as stated by the customer. These expectations are often expressed in subjective terms that may not be directly measurable by objective criteria.

Bibliography

Albrecht, Karl, and Ron Zemke. *Service America! Doing Business in the New Economy*. Homewood, IL: Dow Jones-Irwin, 1985.

Bright, James R. "Strategy and Tactics in Innovation," proceedings of the Portland Technology Management Conference, Portland, OR, October 1991.

Camp, Robert C. "Benchmarking: The Search for Industry Best Practices that Lead to Superior Performance." *Quality Progress*, May 1989, 66–68.

Cary, Mark, Bonnie Kay, Paul Orleman, Wayne Robertshaw, Gabriel Ross, David Saunders, Wallace Wallace, and John Wittenbraker. "The Customer Window." *Quality Progress*, June 1987, 37–42.

Crosby, Philip. *Quality Improvement Through Defect Prevention: The Individual's Role*. Suttercreek, CA: Crosby Associates, Inc., 1985.

———. *Quality Is Free: The Art of Making Quality Certain*. New York: McGraw-Hill, 1979.

Deming, W. Edwards., *Out of the Crisis*. Cambridge, MA: Massachusetts Institute of Technology Center for Advanced Engineering Study, 1986.

————. *Quality, Productivity, and Competitive Position*. Cambridge, MA: Massachusetts Institute of Technology Center for Advanced Engineering Study, 1982.

DePree, Max. *Leadership Is an Art*. New York: Doubleday, 1989.

Drucker, Peter F. *Management Tasks, Responsibilities, Practices*. New York: Harper & Row Publishers, Inc., 1973.

Fuchsberg, Gilbert. "Quality Programs Show Shoddy Results." *Wall Street Journal*, May 14, 1992.

Fukuda, Ryuji. *Managerial Engineering: Techniques for Improving Quality and Productivity in the Workplace*. Cambridge, MA: Productivity, Inc., 1983

Hauser, John R., and Don Clausing. "The House of Quality." *Harvard Business Review*, May–June 1988, 63–73.

Havener, Clifton L. *Value Based Business*. Forest Lake, MN: Growth Resources Group, Inc., 1990.

Ishikawa, Kaoru. *What Is Total Quality Control? The Japanese Way*. Englewood Cliffs, NJ: Prentice-Hall, Inc., 1984.

Juran, Joseph M. *Juran on Planning for Quality*. New York: Free Press, Collier Macmillan, 1988.

Kenny, Andrew A. "A New Paradigm for Quality Assurance." *Quality Progress*, June 1988, 30–32.

King, Robert. "Listening to the Voice of the Customer: Using the Quality Function Deployment System." *National Productivity Review*, Summer 1987, 277–281.

Lawton, Robin L. "Applying Customer-Centered Quality to Human Resources." *National Productivity Review*, Summer 1992, 393–404.

————. "Creating a Customer-Centered Culture." *Quality Forum*, March 1991, 5–9.

————. "Creating a Customer-Centered Culture in Service Industries." *Quality Progress*, September 1991, 69–72.

————. "Creating Total Customer Satisfaction: A Service Quality Strategy that Will Work for You." *Quality and Participation*, June 1992, 38–44.

Lowry, Karen. "Can This Hot-Rodder Make Honda Racy Again?" *Business Week*, July 9, 1990, 58–59.

Nadler, Gerald, and Shozo Hibino, *Breakthrough Thinking*. Rocklin, CA: Prima Publishing, 1990.

McCarroll, Thomas. "The Supply-Side Scourge." *Time*, November 13, 1989, 81.

Machiavelli, Niccolo. *The Prince*. New York: The New American Library of World Literature, Inc., 1952.

Parasuraman, A., L. L. Berry, and V. A. Zeithaml. "Understanding Customer Expectations of Service." *Sloan Management Review*, Spring 1991, 39–48.

Peters, Tom, and Robert Waterman. *In Search of Excellence*. New York: Harper & Row Publishers, Inc., 1982.

Schwartz, M. H. "A Question of Semantics." *Quality Progress*, November 1991, 59–63.

Senge, Peter M. "The Leader's New Work: Building Learning Organizations." *Sloan Management Review*, Fall 1990, 7–23.

Stalk, George. "Time—The Next Source of Competitive Advantage." *Harvard Business Review*, July–August 1988, 41–51.

Stalk, George, Jr., and Thomas M. Hout. *Competing Against Time: How Time-Based Competition Is Reshaping Global Markets*. New York: The Free Press, 1990.

Sullivan, L. P. "The Seven Stages in Company-Wide Quality Control." *Quality Progress*, May 1986, 77–83.

Taguchi, Genichi, and Don Clausing. "Robust Quality." *Harvard Business Review*, January–February 1990, 65–73.

Wollner, George E. "The Law of Producing Quality." *Quality Progress*, January 1992, 35–40.

Index